catalyst for adventure

The True Story of Best Friends Traveling Through Europe

crystal stanczak

PublishAmerica
Baltimore

First printing

ISBN: 1-4137-6042-2
PUBLISHED BY PUBLISHAMERICA, LLLP
www.publishamerica.com
Baltimore

Printed in the United States of America

dedication

Thank you to Jesus, Mom, Dad, Gabrielle, Rachel, and Phil, for all of your support through my crazy whims. And thanks to Vicki and Summer for the inspiration. Philippians 1:6.

portland, oregon, u.s.a.

At first glance, the looped thread in a cubicle is often mistaken for gray. However, when one spends endless hours staring at the ergonomically-correct cage, it becomes evident that someone in China loomed highlights of purple and red in with the gray. This may have been a corporate decision, based on millions of dollars worth of studies that indicate, "Workers who see bits of color throughout the day are more productive." My company was truly benefitting from those bits of color on the wall of my cubicle. I was one of the most productive hamsters running the wheel for the corporate agenda.

For five years of college and graduate school, professors spouted at me speeches that began with, "When you are in the 'real world' …" and "Things won't be the same outside of college, because …" Like a fawn I innocently heeded their advice, fearing this "real world," hoping, somehow, to conquer it. It wasn't until I was knee-deep in paper shredding, next to a sterile-smelling copy machine, that I realized—professors are full of crap. These slightly pudgy, balding men with halitosis talked a hard game, but logically, I deduced in the copy room, they had no authority to speak about the real world. In all probability, they had been professional students for ten years, and then spent the rest of their lives trying to break into the college scene once again, this time on the other side of the podium. Betrayal filled my soul. If ever I were a college professor I would have the guts to tell students the truth:

"There is no such thing as the 'real world.' Life outside of college is the same, only you work more and can finally afford an oil change."

All of the work and wonder produced by my college career had driven me into the heart of a boring job where I spent my days helping ungrateful burnouts with their financial accounts. My life revolved around precious weekends, which were mostly spent helping my best friend, Summer, plan her upcoming wedding.

The dresses were ordered. Princess-cut with spaghetti straps and wine shimmer. Summer was to be married in four months and she had chosen these gowns to match her cream-colored number. As maid of honor, I had the responsibility of checking sizes for the other girls and helping to host various pre-matrimony events.

Summer and Sam had been college sweethearts. They met at a small school in a small town, and fell in love over homemade meals in her small apartment. Like most couples, Summer and Sam had their kinks. In fact, they were involved in two relationship-counseling groups. As Summer's roommate, I often had the pleasure of learning the right "trigger words" to make my non-existent mate feel understood. (Such knowledge, I was sure, would be useful if I ever found someone who didn't bore me to death.)

The more counseling Summer and Sam attended, the more

evident their mismatch became, so, it was as a relieved shock one night that Summer opened our apartment door in tears.

"It's over," she sobbed. "I broke up with Sam."

This was not the first time they had broken up.

"It is really over?" I questioned.

She nodded with an assurance as stable as concrete. And it was. Halfway into the planning of a large wedding, Summer had the courage to call it off.

Losing your first love is like Taco Bell. It is one of those half-spoon-half-fork utensils grating at your completely exposed heart with the vigor of a fat kid trying to reach the bottom of his refried beans. It is closing your eyes with open arms to embrace a sweet future only to be smacked down by a Mac truck. Given the option, I would rather be hit by the truck.

In times like that, one can only try and survive. Summer, like anyone who has been in love, had become an amputee overnight. Sure, she could walk, but a piece inside of her was gone and it would never grow back. As her friend, I would not try to feed her the generic speech that says, "There are other fish in the sea," or "I guess it just wasn't meant to be." I knew full well that the breakup had altered her life forever.

My uncle was a quadriplegic. After his accident, he could not move his limbs. They shrank in atrophy until he merely had twigs in a wheelchair. He did, however, adapt. He began using his teeth to paint. In my youth, I often admired his careful brush strokes that caused a vase to glow on canvas. More so, I admired the Vietnam soldier who, despite having to drink through a long straw, became the best painter I knew. Like my uncle, Summer would adapt. She would live on without part of her heart and even find new talents, gifts, and strengths. This was the time to discover what the world could offer. She was picking up the pieces of a would-be life, and I was dying to leave the shackles of my life that was. In one evening, the road toward a husband, new car, house, and family acquired a fork. Something else was out there. We both anxiously listed the possibilities, not fully realizing that heartache is the best catalyst for adventure.

Summer took the next few days off from work. We walked the streets of downtown Portland, discussing the shock of the break up. It was obvious that she was devastated for hurting Sam.

"Sam was an innocent bystander of my confusion. I was so caught up in planning a wedding that I neglected to plan my life," she said.

"Well," I offered, "he would have gotten more hurt if this happened any later."

She nodded. I wished that I could take away Summer's pain. She did not have the strength to talk much more, so we sat in silence, watching two backpackers catch a city train. Thinking back, I'm under the impression that these fellows were angels. Unlike stereotypical backpackers, the young men were clean and attractive. They both had dreadlocks and carried guitars, making an impression that lingered until the next day, when Summer's mother, Elizabeth, joined us for lunch.

"Summer," Elizabeth said. "I think you should take time off from life. After all, you almost got married. Your entire life has changed paths … maybe you should do something big, like … go backpacking through Europe."

Elizabeth had no knowledge of the striking twenty-something backpackers that we had seen the day before. Summer squinted, thinking intensely about her mother's proposal. Backpacking would force her to reflect upon what she really wanted, it would open her eyes to the world, and she'd find out where she fit in.

Summer looked at me and asked," Crystal, do you want to backpack through Europe for like four months or something?"

At that point, I would have done anything to make Summer feel better. Leaving the country would take her mind off of Sam and give me a break from the cookie-cutter life I had been chasing since I graduated from high school.

It took me all of thirty seconds to respond with, "Yeah, sure. Why not?"

We would, in the next six months, save all of our money, quit our jobs, move out of our apartment, kiss our friends and family goodbye, and venture into the unknown.

A sea of maps and guidebooks were sprawled across the floor as Summer and I worked on our fifth itinerary. The topic at hand—whether or not Greece was an option. Seeing that I had never been to Greece, it was difficult for me to know what I was giving up if we didn't go. Making itineraries was almost as enjoyable as looking at maps. Until this point, I usually stared at maps of the United States because in college I took road trips to most of the southern and western states, and it was fun to find the little towns where I filled my gas tank. Now, the map-looking had evolved onto another continent, improving my geography and ability to be a smart global citizen.

"Well, maybe we should decide on Greece later," Summer concluded, as the phone rang.

Smiling, I agreed and went to investigate the audacious phone call that bothered us in the middle of a planning session. My little sister was on the line. She was quiet and uttered to me a secret that had been tearing her up inside. Since I was three, I had always considered my little sister to be my baby. When life at home was tough, I was strong for her. Following my instinct, I waited until I hung up the phone to feel anything.

"My parents are getting divorced," I stated to Summer.

My stomach began to turn just thinking about it. Every person in my family would be affected by the trauma, the gravity of it all. In a few months, my parents would no longer be married. That reality sent chills up the top of my arms and zapped my neck, hovering in my chest. My mouth held despair in all of its gloomy weight. If I knew the right word to scream, I would have said it, but instead I just swallowed the despair, letting it thud into my chest once more.

Maybe this was not the time to be the rock in my family. Any one of my friends could point out that I was the emotionally stable one—the "nice" sister. In the small town where I grew up, people knew to count on me if they needed a referee or a gentle answer. Storms were calmed by my very words, and I learned early to mask my own hurt feelings for the benefit of my loved ones. How would my family manage while I was overseas?

Five months later we were snowed in. Portland was entirely shut down, so I drove to work jealous of anyone who got to stay home and shovel. One sixth of our employees showed up to work, and lucky for the few of us that did, we were sent home with pay. Summer worked for the state, and it is common knowledge that state workers get everything off. If Oregon was mourning the loss of an old hippie musician, the state workers would be sent home to watch *Judge Judy*. Jack Frost not only helped our veg-fest; he also opened time for us to plan for the European Backpacking Extravaganza. I bought a passport, plane ticket, money belt, Eurail pass, wardrobe, and a car shammy that would serve as a compact towel. At that point, there in the cozy apartment, being paid to do nothing, life did not seem too bad.

For two weeks, Summer and I tried to use up all of the groceries in our cupboards, making meals out of oatmeal and canned green beans. We would be moving out of the apartment, and I quit my job early to work on the packing. Leaving my job was scary. The future was uncertain, and it was reckless for me to just take off. Stress mounted as we moved out of our cute place on Troy Street. Within a week I went to an out-of-town wedding, set up twelve meetings for my part time job, went to four meetings, entertained my mother from Texas, did my taxes, packed up everything that I owned, moved my junk into storage, cleaned the apartment (so as to get our deposit back), and in the process, broke down in tears—right in the middle of a fast food chain. Every part of me was beat. I could hardly find myself behind the dark cloud of negativity. There were so many things to worry about, and I looked forward to the months ahead where I could leave all my continental baggage behind me.

england

You cannot chose your row-mates when on a long distance flight, so it is always an anxious time when forcing your way down the narrow row, squinting to find seat 40J. The 777 was an endless hallway of screaming kids and British people on their way back from a holiday. It seemed that all the Brits were way cooler, smarter, beautiful, and altogether chic than we humble Americans. Foreign accents flooded the aircraft. In the presence of such company I suddenly noticed how harsh my accent was, how graceless my carriage was, and how round my face was. I felt judged and conscious of the uncouth manner in which I behaved, and hoped that I would not be stuck next to a haughty old lady for nine hours. At least Summer thought I was cool.

Our row neighbor, Bob, ended up being fairly normal, aside from the fact that he whistled uncontrollably and without regard to the hundred people in his audible range. Unlike most male strangers, Bob projected a completely non-threatening air. This, we later found out, was because he was as gay as a chorus line. He was on route to Rotterdam, Netherlands, for a man with whom he had had a three-day fling.

"So where are you from?" Summer asked Bob.

"Toronto, eh. I'm going on holiday. What are you guys doing?" Bob asked.

"We're going to backpack around Europe for three and a half months," Summer answered with twinkling eyes.

"That's a long time, eh. Why did you decide to do that?" He inquired.

"Adventure," Summer said.

"Excitement," I added.

"Expensive," Bob declared with a smile.

He was right. This was expensive. Yet somehow I knew that it would be worth it. My brother once told me, "Crystal, worry about the money later, because when you're eighty, you'd pay a million dollars to be twenty-three and in Europe." He also told me, "Don't trust Whitey!" My brother took a year off of work to explore the world, and I respected his advice. Without regret, I watched the Statue of Liberty wave us goodbye, the last piece of the United States we would see for three and a half months.

Our first steps in London were an awestruck stupor.

Summer was grinning from ear to ear when she stated the obvious, "We're in London, Crystal!"

Before closing her mouth, she realized that browsing around the airport was not a good idea since there were British locals walking slowly in front of her. She crashed right into a blond boy who refused to acknowledge her Yankee apology. When we got to the customs counter, a female agent gave me the third-degree-hairy-eyeball combination. She interrogated me like a criminal, and I took too long to answer her questions.

"Why are you in England?" she asked.

"Well," I began, "we're starting this adventure, and I just love England, so I thought that we might as well start here. Plus the airfares aren't too bad, know what I mean?" I said, trying to successfully carry my first local conversation.

"How long will you be here?" the agent asked coldly.

"For three and a half months," I answered, assuming she was asking about our entire trip.

She proceeded to search me for valid documents, making sure that I was not an illegal immigrant. Naïveté was obviously not a desired quality at the London airport.

Our train ride into the city reminded me of an opening scene in a Harry Potter movie. Fog caused gray buildings to disappear. There was no background music in the car, and men wore black and beige as they read newspapers. All of the locals avoided eye contact in a sterile manner that discouraged small talk. The buildings downtown were shorter than I imagined. Eleven million people lived in London, stretched out into suburbs. Vast breadth made up for the city's lack of height. The metropolis reached so far that people had to travel by the underground system called "the tube." As a backpacker, I had no choice but to clunk around everything I had on my back through the subway. This was not acceptable for one man on the tube, who actually glared at my backpack and made a scene by scoffing and switching seats on our train. Summer and I quickly learned that when commuting in London, you must know the social rules. You must stand to the right, walk with a purpose, know your exit, look no one in the eye, mind your head, mind the gap, say "sorry" when you bump into someone, "cheers" when someone lets you pass, and always respect the queue (the line). Once we understood the rules, the city was amazing.

We invited our airplane row-mate, Bob, to join us for a day of exploration as we toured the Tower of London. Any initial frigidity I had previously felt melted away when one of the older workers at the Tower gave us a personal thirty-minute tour. He taught us everything we wanted to know about Henry the Eighth, including the juicy details of his love life.

"Did you *know*," our friendly tour guide began, "that Enry the Eifph wrote the song 'Greensleeves'?"

"Wow!" Summer said. "Terrific! I love that song. How does it go again?"

The man hummed "Greensleeves," even closing his eyes during a triumphant crescendo. This was the noble, imperial London that I had anticipated. It would be the first of many days that I would declare, "Today is the best day of my life."

The next day we took in the Tate Modern Museum. After an exhausting look at countless explicit images, we sat in the museum wondering why they call a naked man frolicking in a cube *art*.

"Summer," I asked, "would I be totally unrefined if I said that I didn't like this stuff?"

"No, Crystal, and there is a reason," Summer explained. "Art is supposed to provoke an emotional reaction. It is easier to provoke disgust or violation than hope or delight. I think that modern art uses graphic nudity and chaos to make the viewer feel sick."

"That's a cheap way to get a reaction," I said.

"Definitely," Summer replied. " I much prefer the Italian artist, Carravagio. He uses dark tones in his paintings to create mysterious beauty. When I look at his work, I feel intrigued and happy." That day in London, Summer discovered that she didn't like modern art. There is some kind of power that comes with knowing which kind of art you like. Part of Summer's individuality had declared independence from popular opinion.

"Let's get out of here," Summer said. "If I have to look at any more of this crap I might get sick."

We left the Tate Modern, never to return.

Later, we went on a historical walking tour of London, presented by my favorite tour guide, Judy. Judy was direct, flawless in her presentation, and had a teensy threshold for background noise.

"Here we have the church of John Wesley," Judy began. "Is anyone here a *Methodist*?"

"No, very *well then*. If you would just cross the *street* and …" She turned to scold some noisy local children, "*Where* is your *mother*. *Have* you no *decency*?"

Both her irritation and her information made for an engaging tour. To my delight, she randomly took us by the Guildhall School of Music and Drama. One really wonderful English actor studied there, Orlando Bloom. As I am given to periodic celebrity crushes, it was providence that we happened past this school, where the love of my life spent several years studying. Most girls outgrow impossible celebrity crushes, but not us. Summer wrote postcards to the Joe Nichol's fan club and I insisted on being called Mrs. Bloom. Fantasizing about our famous men kept us from dating losers. Besides, Orlando (or as I like to call him, "Lando"), was too perfect to ignore—he was handsome, heartfelt, and had an irresistible English accent.

All of our sightseeing added to Summer's jetlag, and she turned in early, while I went to observe things in the market across the street. The deli sandwiches came in such Euro-gourmet flavors as Brie with granny smith apple and grape, or celery and cheddar, or cucumber. Sparkling water in hand, I went to pay the checkout lady (who might as well have been speaking a foreign language for the thickness of her accent). My sandwich cost 1£90 … almost $4.00 American. With prices like that, we'd end up saving money by fasting and consuming the jam and bread that our hostel provided, hopefully not getting scurvy in the process.

Sitting on a step, I watched thin, stylish people pass. The men were so hot! They were lean with perfectly styled hair, and wore purple dress shirts with purple ties. The women wore little makeup and always a touch of Burberry. At that point I was glad that I had splurged on a Burberry scarf. "Sweet Home Alabama" boomed from the bar across the street and I wondered if I was the only person within a ten-mile radius who had actually been to Alabama.

After a good rest, we went to Harrods department store. Harrods was exhilarating, yet disheartening at the same time. We would wander from the sushi department, into the fine jewelry department, amazed at the easy transition from fish to diamonds—something that only Harrods could pull off.

"I was just looking at a tuna roll, wondering what it would taste like, and four steps later, I am gawking at engagement rings. How weird is that?" Summer observed.

"Yeah," I replied, as we walked into the next room—a tea parlor.

The shiny displays were a feast to behold, and sorrowfully, they reminded us that backpackers cannot afford luxury. Just so we wouldn't leave Harrods discouraged, we sat on the top floor at the plush Georgian Restaurant.

"The bathroom has a paid attendant and perfume," Summer whispered, inviting me to check it out.

"Is there a dress code to use the bathroom here?" I asked sarcastically.

We pretended to be high rollers and ordered eight-dollar coffee from the restaurant, unable to afford anything else. If, in the future, I returned to Harrods with money, I vowed to order a twenty-dollar sandwich to go with my eight-dollar coffee.

Feeling our poverty, it was an inopportune time to meet Christian, our roommate in the hostel. Christian was a Connecticut Ivy-league brat, raised by generations of New England's old money. He took time off from college to gallivant around Europe on his father's tab. Summer and I pegged him right from the start, and it was not because he talked about private school, penny loafers, or sailing. What gave Christian away was his flippant carriage. It was obvious that he had never had to worry about a thing in his life. Meeting people from outside our backgrounds gave Summer and I a greater sense of who we were.

Any outsider might mistake Summer for a rich kid, like Christian. Only a few favored friends knew that Summer had worked arduously for her bachelor's degree and her job with the state legislature. Summer came from a single-parent home and could not imagine having the world served to her on a silver platter. This vulnerable detail was painful and risky for her to share, but I could see in her eyes the peace that comes with showing authenticity to a trustworthy friend.

Before we left London, Summer and I decided to see a musical.

"I heard that *The Lion King* was good," Summer said, looking at the theater listings.

"Oh wow!" I said, noticing another show. "We have to see

Anything Goes! I was in that musical in high school, and trust me, it's so funny!"

"Do you really want to see it?" Summer asked.

"Yes, absolutely, and you do too!" I convinced Summer.

My mind drifted back eight years and suddenly I was a wild freshman tap dancing on a familiar stage. Our cast listened to the audience cheer as we hit perfect steps in our flapper dresses. On the rainy streets of London, I realized that dancing had slowly ceased to be important to me, and I was sad.

Summer interrupted my thoughts, "Sure, let's see it."

As we stepped into the theater a few hours later, I hoped that the cast would do the play justice—and they did. For two hours, we watched superbly coordinated dance numbers and well delivered American accents. *Anything Goes* followed zany passengers in the 1920s on a cruise ship from the United States to England, so it fit our circumstance well—aside from the flapper dresses, of course. The lead character sang a love song as smooth as caramel, and we both fell in love with him. After watching *Anything Goes*, Summer would finally recognize the songs that I belted out in the shower.

"It's delightful, It's delicious, It's delovely!" I sang as we stepped onto the theater's plush ruby staircase.

"That was the best musical I've ever seen," Summer said. "It was funny and it had a great plot and adorable characters. I loved it!"

"Me too," I replied, glad that she enjoyed the play that was so close to my heart. After such a performance I promised myself that I would dance again.

Our next plan was to rent a car, learn to drive on the other side of the road, and travel to Bath, an ancient roman city, and then to the Cotswolds, a series of villages that had sprung up by a boom in the woolen industry. Renting the car was the easy part—with a swipe of Summer's Visa, we were handed the keys. The hard part was managing the other side of the road. It took us back seven years. Summer was suddenly a newly licensed teenager, strangling the steering wheel with her nose pressed up against the windshield. As a passenger, it was difficult for me to relinquish control. Summer was doing better than I would, and yet I still felt my glut muscles tense up each time she almost hit something.

"Summer, look out! A construction worker!" I cried as she nearly killed him.

She looked at me, wanting to yell, but instead erupted into laughter and said, "Well, I didn't hit him, did I?"

After a while, our fragile nerves finally calmed. We were on the open road in a proper Euro-teeny piece of machine. The car had a compact disc player, allowing us to sing country music at the top of our lungs. As usual, we danced around, twisting our hips and jarring our arms as much as we could while in a seated position. This went on for a good while until we encountered a stop sign and an old English couple caught us, mid-boogie.

"And I will sail my vessel," I sang to them from the car.

It was evident that they were not Garth Brooks fans. Our activity switched on and off, like a game of musical chairs, stopping each time we hit a red light. Cars are one of the few places left in the world where you can truly express yourself.

We opted for a western route that took us past London suburbs and the English Channel. One mile had us driving alongside the beach at Brighton where kids gleefully rode a seafront ferris wheel and old fishermen looked for crabs. If my father were there, no doubt he'd be asking the other fishermen what they were catching that day. Summer turned the heat up in our car so that we could roll down the windows and smell the sea air. It was salty and periodically blew gusts of cotton candy and popcorn. Pleased, we photographed the scene and drove a while longer. The sun was setting over rural England, inviting us to pull over and watch orange fade to pink.

"God must have known that the dark of night is sometimes depressing," I said to Summer, "and maybe the only way to transition into it is to lure us with a sunset."

"And maybe the only way to get our lazy butts up in the morning is to lure us with a sunrise," Summer added.

"Touché," I replied. "Although, I can't remember the last time I saw a sunrise. I'm too cranky to appreciate them."

"Yeah," Summer said, "you are cranky in the morning."

"Hey! I resent that!" I responded. "I'm also cranky in the mid-afternoon!"

There, on a loose gravel road, Summer and I traveled back to a simpler time, when humble country folks mended fences and tipped their hats to ladies. Before we knew it, darkness had enveloped the land, and we were lost. A quarter tank of gas was burned in the city of Bath as we desperately searched for our youth hostel. Directions were bleak and every corner had an identical roundabout to brave. The roads were narrow, and with each stride we faced the threat of scraping a parked car. Summer and I switched positions a few times as rage mounted.

The only verbal exchange between us was a series of irritated sighs until she emphatically bellowed, "Forget Bath! I hate Bath!"

"Yeah, Bath sucks! I hate it!" I concurred.

We took turns listing all of the things we hated about the abashing city until our anger lifted into entertainment.

"Bath is dirty and full of losers!" I said.

"Yeah, what kind of a town doesn't have street signs?" Summer agreed.

"I'll tell you why they don't have street signs," I said, "because the locals are illiterate."

"I heard that Ozzy Osborne is the mayor of Bath," Summer added. "He makes his cabinet get high with him before they make city plans and road construction."

"That explains why we've just passed the Ye Old Ale House for the third time," I said.

Summer honked the horn in protest and I hit the window, startling an old man on his way into the Ye Old Ale House. Since we weren't tired, and since our car was nice and toasty, we decided to skip Bath and go to the Cotswolds early.

At 11:30 p.m., without gas to spare, our wee machine had arrived in Stow-on-the-Wold, a shepherding community in the middle of nowhere. It was fascinating to see how this town kept simple living intact. The buildings had thatched roofs, window signs were handmade, and nothing was open past 9:00 p.m. We were truly delighted by Stow-on-the-Wold until we realized that we had come too late to check into a hostel.

Summer suggested, "Well, we *do* have a car. Why don't we just sleep in here?"

"Yeah, okay, we'll save ourselves thirty bucks," I responded.

That seemed logical enough. After all, it was warm and we were not large girls. Now, sleeping in the car is an economical idea, void of many threats in, say, July. However, this was February. More than that, this was February in England. Not an hour had gone by until every ounce of warm air had been vacuumed right out of the car. Our cozy Euromobile was now a miserable icebox. Summer and I spent the night brainstorming about how to stay warm—we tried extra clothes, periodic car heating, and even cuddling while the emergency break jabbed us. The Cotswolds were uniquely pretty, but we could not fully appreciate them in our homeless state. This lasted into the next day as Summer had poor circulation and couldn't feel her feet until noon.

In these interrelated towns called the Cotswolds, the residents take time each year to walk the grounds between fields in order to keep them in the public domain. It is legal to saunter through someone's backyard until you reach the next town. Despite our sleepless night, Summer and I had ourselves one of these amazing ten-mile strolls. Landscapes of fields in many hues of green rolled into petite villages where houses boasted golden-gray brick. They didn't have addresses, and instead were known by their names, such as Heather Cottage or Sussex House. Little arrows directed us through gates of all kinds, and sheep greeted us around each bend.

"Would you ever live in England?" I asked Summer.

"I don't know. I think I'd miss home too much," she responded. "I wouldn't want to live as an absentee aunt."

"I would live here," I stated. "The people are so funny and interesting, with that dry sarcastic humor."

"I could see you living here," she said. "You've already moved more than anyone else I know. How many times have you moved again?"

"Eighteen. Moving is my way of life. My parents are like gypsies. They change states more often than their socks," I said.

"I forgot, is your dad in the military or something?" she asked.

"Witness protection program. No I'm just kidding—he's an engineer. Moving is just what my family does. Picking up and going isn't scary to me, you know?" I said.

"Is sticking in one place scary?" she asked me.

"I don't know," I said.

Walking in the country has a way of bringing up important issues. Maybe staying in one place, getting too attached to a group of people or a home, did scare me. Our ten miles passed effortlessly, as we hashed out this issue and many others.

"How does your family argue?" I asked Summer.

"That's a strange question," she said.

"Well these are the kind of questions you have time to answer on a ten-mile stroll through the English countryside," I explained. "Anyway, I like to hear how different people argue so that I know how to get along with them."

"I get it," Summer said. "My family just says whatever they feel like saying. No one is afraid to share his or her opinion. Like, my sister will say, 'Summer that color looks horrible on you, you should never wear it again.'"

"Doesn't that hurt your feelings?" I asked, being sensitive myself.

"I am just used to it," Summer said, and then a few minutes later, "Actually, yes, it does hurt my feelings."

Some sheep were eavesdropping on our conversation— maybe they needed a lesson in conflict too.

The only thing that made our afternoon more English was high tea at a prissy tea room, where we enjoyed corner sandwiches and scones with clotted cream. After such a lunch, I became obsessed with whipping cream, and would continue to work at fluffing my own with a fork during future meals.

England impressed me. The silly social rules, the diverse styles of living, and the way they sang their words, causing even statements to sound like questions.

One young man, Allister, once told me, "I *enjoy* the

American drink called *Mountain Dew*."

If I could carry my words so delicately, I would, but the English accent is a piano that I play like a man without fingers. English folks had won a soft spot in my heart, and I knew that leaving for Ireland was not the end of my English experience. For the rest of my life I would enjoy Hugh Grant movies and return to Heathrow airport whenever I could afford to do so.

ireland

We were safe and sound in Dublin, having our share of Guinness and strolls along the friendly city. Summer enjoyed pleasant conversations with people from Wales, Switzerland, and even Iowa—hooray for Dubuque, Iowa. I was still on the lookout for Bono in Dublin. My best guess was that he'd be outside of a trendy bar, wearing his famous shades and singing "Sunday Bloody Sunday" aloud. That way I could instantly recognize him and make marital arrangements for he and my older sister, in the event that both of their spouses died.

The people of Ireland were accepting. Coming from England, where black was the most popular color, I felt free to express myself. Sometimes people would ask me for directions because they thought I was Irish. Surprisingly, I was one of the few redheads around. One other was a lap dancer who stayed at our hostel.

Summer and I liked to make small talk with our neighbors. We'd make friends and go to movies or cathedrals with people from all over the world. Likewise, I intended to befriend my fellow redhead as I engaged her in light discussion.

"Hi, I'm Crystal. What's your name?" I asked.

"My name is Collette, and I am from France." Detecting my accent she continued, "French people hate Americans."

"It's nice to meet you too," I replied. "So what do you do?"

"I am a lap dancer," she responded.

How should I respond to that? Seedy strip joints were not places that I spent much time. In fact, I couldn't well relate to a girl who made a living by letting sweaty old perverts see her naked.

Not wanting Collette to feel judged, I said the only thing I could think of: "So what kind of a man would pay to …"

Every word stung worse than the previous one. Collette was unintentionally berated while I stuck my foot harder into my mouth. At that point I could taste the salt on my shoelaces.

"Stop talking. Just stop," I told myself as I tried to dig my way out of verbal quicksand.

That night Collette and three of her friends stumbled into the room at 3:00 a.m., sloppy drunk. A Scottish guy was yelling as the girls cackled at him.

This went on for an hour until Summer marched over to them and said with hostility, "It is 4:00 a.m., and some of us are trying to sleep here!"

They stopped yelling, but I did not sleep soundly for the fear that the Scottish guy would kill me in my sleep. It was a good thing we would be leaving Dublin next day because I dared not face the wrath of Collette and her friends in the midst of their horrendous hangovers.

Among best friends, there is an invisible code of conduct. Rule number one: If a friend ever asks you, "Do I look fat?"

you cannot, under any circumstance, tell her "Yes, you look like Mama Cass after Thanksgiving turkey." In that situation, the best thing to do is merely pick out another outfit for her, offer a little self-deprecation (example: "I am so unhappy with my butt these days."), and suggest for the both of you to go on a run. As tender as the "fat" subject is, there is one even more delicate—one that can shatter the tightest bond between girlfriends—men. Rule number two: If best friends are interested in the same man, both should avoid being alone with him.

So it was, on a crisp Irish morning, Summer and I met the ultimate test of the bonds of friendship—Patrick. Patrick, like most Irish men, was not the most aesthetically pleasing specimen. In fact, without a cool haircut and cute jeans, he might have been borderline homely. However, when he started talking, your attention, and your heart, belonged to him.

Taking numerous suggestions from our fellow backpackers, Summer and I were about to venture on a six-day roving Irish bus tour. Patrick was our official tour guide, and the moment we boarded his bus, I saw his eyes lock on each girl like an arrogant honing device. His confidence was a force of nature, causing me to stop in my tracks while he blew me over like a trailer in a hurricane.

"That, over there, is a fairy tree." Patrick said. "The Irish are very superstitious."

"As the story goes, a great farmer once forfeited his life in Ireland because he fell in love with a fairy. He joined the fairy in eternity and left the land to rot, thus causing the potato famine," he told our group.

He had all kinds of information about Ireland. We hung on his every word, and now, thinking back, I understand that he could have been blabbering whatever came to his inventive mind—his perfectly messy hair indicated that he had a great imagination. The rhythm in his speech was precise yet easy, and he used profanity in every sentence.

"You look like a regular Irish Colleen." Patrick said as he flipped one of my tresses.

"Well," I explained, "my great grandfather on my mom's side was from Cork."

"Lots of Americans come over here as if it is their mother land or something," Patrick said. "We call them plastic Paddys. They cry when they get off of the plane and kiss the blarney stone and all of that, like."

"Do you think all of us are like that?" I asked, hoping that he didn't have a bad impression of me.

"Maybe not the lot of you," he answered.

Our tour took us to splendid Irish countryside, where stone walls divided plots of land into long rows. Jaw-dropping cliffs lined the sea as a warning to enemies who tried to come to Ireland by the Atlantic. Quirky little towns were inhabited by generations of families and a thousand cozy pubs. With a busload of instant friends and good Irish stout, it was easy to get swept away. For six days, Ireland might as well have been the only country in existence, and Patrick, for that matter, might as well have been the only guy in existence. He'd take us to magnificent viewpoints by day and low-light music halls by night. He called every girl "baby" and commanded an invisible spotlight. It was special just to be near him.

Instead of flirting with Patrick, I always did my best to match his wit. He'd tell an interesting story, and I'd come up with a quick one-liner that made him chuckle, to which he'd respond with an even quicker retort that made me laugh uncontrollably. This silly, clever, walking pint of Guinness had me wrapped around his finger.

Each day I'd divide my time between basking in glorious landscapes and thinking of things I could say to Patrick that might leave an impression. Simple arithmetic told me that I was one of a hundred cute girls he would meet that year alone, and to impress him the way he impressed me was quite a feat. It wasn't long before I noticed that I was not the only girl hypnotized by Patrick.

Summer and I were seated right up front, asking each other silly questions.

"If you had to eat someone on the bus, who would it be?" Summer asked.

"I guess the girl from Austria," I told Summer. "She looks like she could feed the entire bus for awhile. Alright, now my question, would you rather date a guy who had chronic diarrhea breath or a obscenely long back hair?

"I'm gonna go with back hair," she replied, and then out of the blue she asked me, "Do you have a crush on Patrick?"

He was clearly in audible range. Did I admit it right there? My hands glistened. My throat lumped.

"Yeah," I said, trying to be aloof. "Doesn't everybody? Don't you?"

"Yes, I do," she replied.

Oh crap. She did too. My loyalties were torn between my own heart and my best friend. Throughout my life when this situation arose, I had always immediately retracted my feelings for the guy in question. Eighties girl-power sitcoms propagated my deep-seeded conviction that guys should never come between friends. It had always been easier for me to swallow the bitter pill of unspoken attraction than to lose a friend. This time would be no different. Summer and I stopped asking each other silly questions after that. We bumped along the front seat in silence. Patrick, though not directly involved in our conversation, kept silent as well.

At 7:00 p.m., the little youth hostel in Killarney was buzzing with activity. A cloud of hairspray choked the hallway as Summer and I searched through our clothes as if we were backstage at a beauty pageant. Patrick had arranged for the entire tour to watch live traditional music at a club in town, and everyone was primping up for the event. This was a red-lipstick night.

My hair was ironed and chic, perfect for the gorgeous black heels on my feet. These heels were too beautiful not to buy, and also too beautiful to comfortably wear for more than an hour. As we walked into the club, I forgot the nuisance of my feet and the throbbing of my freshly plucked eyebrows. My mind was busy creating scenarios in which I would make Patrick notice me.

A bunch of the girls from our tour were already sitting around chatting. Summer and I were almost lost in the giggling when Patrick made his way right in between us.

"Hey, baby," he stated.

Who was he there to see? And did I really like him that much anyway? Had I spent an hour getting ready just to impress an Irish ladies man? At that moment it felt like Patrick was a white net, and girls were too often just a bunch of players volleying around him with tennis rackets. Summer was not my competition. She would never be. She was my friend during a hard breakup, a new life (when my gypsy parents moved us out of state again), and now, during my parent's divorce. There, with Irish fiddles humming in my ears, I put my racket down, and left the club. Maybe Patrick liked me. Maybe he didn't.

Either way, I would not be a part of the competition. I expected Summer to follow suit, and went to sleep with a clear conscience.

The next day our tour bus curled around windy back roads, which gave the large Austrian girl behind me extra incentive to discuss her throbbing hangover. More than the ever-present threat of being puked on, there was a strange tension in the air.

Summer stayed quiet for forty-five minutes until, with a half-smile she said, "Patrick and I kissed last night."

I wanted to crawl under my seat. Embarrassed by my crush or betrayed by my unreciprocated gesture of loyalty the night before, all I could muster was, "Oh … did you have fun?"

I didn't want the details. Summer had broken rule number two of the unspoken girlfriend code of conduct, and I couldn't handle the details until my hurt feelings went away.

Knowing that I didn't need to impress Patrick, my attention was not divided that day. For the first time in Ireland, tumbling hills of green grass danced with me, tempting me to roll over them like a five-year-old. Charismatic old folks charmed me into taking their pictures. Brightly painted buildings had me comparing periwinkle and goldenrod as if I was picking out paint samples. Pasty children in Catholic school uniforms led me to quaint trinket shops. Ireland had me all to itself, and I enjoyed its cheerful whims like never before.

A few hours later I got the details of Summer and Patrick's kiss—uneventful, forced, and now, accompanied by awkwardness. It was an experience of which I was relieved to only be a third party. Then Summer told me something that caused me to melt for her in utter compassion.

"Patrick is the first guy I've kissed since I broke up with Sam last year."

Any hard feelings in me were instantly replaced with

sympathy. She needed say nothing more.

Chelsea, a girl on the tour from Australia, joined Summer and I for a day of window shopping in the adorable town of Kinsale. Since everyone on our tour had found out about Summer and Patrick, girl talk came easily between the three of us. Chelsea was a lawyer, working in London for two years. She was articulate and seemed to have it all together, so I was surprised to find out that she left Australia nursing a broken heart. After spending six years with her fiancé, David, building a life and even a new house, he broke up with her without explanation. He still called her and told her "I love you," which only made the scars worse.

"It was like picking at the scab," she explained, "every time he came to see me and then left again."

"When I broke up with Sam, I just knew it would be better to make it a clean break," Summer said. "Of course there were times that I wanted to call him, but it wasn't fair to either of us."

"I wish that David understood that." Chelsea said. "It's rather selfish really, to keep coming around."

Chelsea understood Summer's life change even better than I could. She inspired Summer with her brave determination to move on.

The sun began to set and we searched for the highest place in Kinsale to take it in. This was on the top a dreadfully steep hill in a new housing development. We broke into the gate and crawled on top of a heap of dirt, without regard to the way it was staining our clothes. There, on the top of the world, Kinsale was dwarf-like. Exhilaration sparkled in each of our eyes, partly due to the gorgeous scene, and partly to the fear that at any point during the event we could have been arrested for trespassing. The town was ancient, and these houses were brand new. This was how most of Europe lived, with one foot in antiquity and the other in post-modernism.

Our last days in Ireland offered us a look into the everyday lives of Dubliners. The tour brought us back to Ireland's largest city where we spent as much time as we could with our new friends. Chelsea, Summer, and I often sat together over a fresh cider, enjoying Irish accents and trading beauty tips.

"I heard that it is bad to wash your hair," Summer said.

"Something about stripping away the natural oils, right?" I asked.

"Yeah, instead of washing our hair, we need to just rinse it and let it condition itself," Summer said.

"I guess I never thought about it," Chelsea replied, then noticing Patrick approaching another table, she said "Oh, look who's trying to talk to the girls from Canada."

Summer was surprised to find Patrick being distant after their encounter. He acted like nothing had happened between them. This is a common practice among guys, one that can crush a girl. When a guy is on the prowl, he makes a girl feel special in order that she let down her guard and let him into her heart. The degree of this varies, depending on such factors as time and the possibility for a future. Just when the girl has decided to trust the prowler enough, he reneges his affections, leaving a laundry list of feelings for the deserted female: confusion, shame, embarrassment, etc. In my life, I have learned to deal with such treatment from guys. In order to survive dating, a girl really has to expect any guy to be guilty of jerk-like tendencies until proven innocent. Maybe this is unfair, but nevertheless, it is a fact. This wisdom was something I was happy to tactfully share with Summer. She had been out of the new relationship world since she met Sam two years earlier, and needed a lesson in defensive dating.

Any American can tell you that a special bond develops

between kids at summer camp. You spend every hour with the same forty other teenagers, doing things that you wouldn't otherwise do in the suburbs (example: riflery, archery and, well, various other forms of weaponry). At night, the cabins become an incubator of self-disclosure. This is because whatever you tell camp people, is not threatened by the fear of the secret resurfacing at a hometown football game. What is said in a cabin stays in a cabin. Also, there is an inevitable camp hook-up phase that occurs within 48 hours of arrival. Pubescent guys and girls find a romance that burns as hot as Phoenix in July, with a person who is probably not even attractive, but their constant presence gives them ten additional cute-points. And so, for a week or two, bonds with these outdoor friends are disproportionately deep. Summer and I did not know until Ireland that the same is true on backpacker bus tours, and, just like the last day of camp, goodbyes are not easy. People exchange email addresses and promise to write. Some even plan to meet up again. We had plans to meet Chelsea in Paris in three days. Having a slight case of post-tour bus depression, the three of us were happy that we could look forward to Paris.

Summer left Ireland knowing that she was worth more than the consolation prize in Patrick's girl-of-the-week contest. With the utmost dignity, she concealed any disappointment that remained within her from the prior week. We were on an Irish ferry sailing away from the Island. The two of us spent the evening trying to avoid drunken creeps from Belfast.

"The English are the scabs on me arse," one man told me, as he shook his beer in my face.

"Would you like a beer?" another guy said to Summer.

"No thanks, that beer tastes bitter," Summer responded.

"Are you trying to say that I slipped something in your beer?" the man shouted. "I resent that accusation."

"No, I'm sorry, I'm not accusing you of anything," Summer said, trying to avoid a beating.

They had hair triggers and insisted upon teaching us how to say "our day will come" in Gaelic. The violent lunacy in their eyes suppressed us from expressing any dissatisfaction we had with the Irish Republican Army. In an attempt to hide, we ended up sleeping on the floor in between semi-reclining chairs. The air was ten degrees too cold, the space in which we tried to sleep was two feet too short, and there was a barnyard smell permeating the air. We concluded that the ship must have been transporting farm animals in the room adjacent to us. It's funny the smells you get used to when you don't have a choice.

france

On the choppy seas, with the smell of decomposed hay in our nostrils, we concentrated on what lay ahead. We were sailing toward the foreign language chapter in our trip. Finally, I would have the chance to use phrases I learned in the five years of French class I had taken.

"Can I use the hall pass to go to the bathroom?" I asked Summer in French.

"I come to school by automobile," I continued.

"I like to eat salad. Do you have two sisters?"

"I went to the store yesterday. My father is not agreeable. The dog is brown."

Yes, this would be a terrific redemption for all of the tiresome hours I had spent conjugating verbs in my French workbook. Maybe the Parisians would also appreciate the Christmas carols I remembered from 11th grade. After all, my rendition of "Frosty the Snowman" was unequivocally the best in the junior class.

Someone once told me, "When you are not looking for love, that's when it finds you." After watching my best friend go through mini-agony, love was that last thing I wanted to find in France. Instead, it found me—three times over.

My first French love came in the form of a hundred-year-old steel structure—the Eiffel Tower. Based on our travel day, I would not have expected to be enchanted that evening. We had had little sleep the night before and were unfamiliar with the Paris subway system. What's worse was that we tried to settle in a hostel during rush hour. When our subway stop had arrived, the car was so packed that Summer couldn't get out. Part of me successfully exited the subway car, and the other part of me (my enormous backpack) did not. The doors shut on my now-ripping backpack, forcing French commuters to push the rest of me out of the car with all of their might. Who ever said that Parisians were not helpful?

With gratitude, I saluted the commuters in their native tongue, "Thank you for your help. I have red hair."

Eventually Summer and I reconnected at our hostel, ecstatic that we could finally take off the thirty-five pounds we'd been hauling on our backs all day. My brother had lent me the same backpack he had used to travel around the world, and I felt a little guilty that this sentimental item was growing into something that I resented.

After a refreshing dinner, we decided that the first tourist attraction we should see was the Eiffel Tower—love at first sight. The occurrence lingers in my soul to this day.

A giddy smile stretched harder across my face the closer my feet took me to the Eiffel Tower. The tower was illuminated in orange tones, and many people stared with upturned heads and dangling jaws ... myself included. In my high school classroom, I had seen this structure a million times, yet somehow in person, there was no comparison. The carefully crafted metal beams represented a dream … and now that I had actually touched it for myself, a photo of the Eiffel tower would never satisfy me. It was much taller than I imagined, surrounded by elegantly manicured botany. Over the noise of street peddlers, I swore that I heard the Seine River singing. On the hour, it put on a ten-minute light show and everyone around ceased discussion, so that the tower would not be offended. With reverence and delight I promised that I would come back. Little did I know that the Eiffel Tower would draw me back every day I spent in Paris.

The next day, Summer and I went shopping at the Champs Elysees. Within fifteen minutes, a classy Asian couple approached us.

"Are you American?" the man asked.

"Yes," I replied.

"We need an American to do us a favor. Can you get this bag?" he said, pointing to a photocopied picture.

They needed two items from the Louis Vitton store, and handed us eight hundred Euro. Summer was bold.

"I'll do it," she said.

"Okay," the man said. "We'll wait for you outside of the store."

Summer had never thrown down that much cash for a handbag, and without fear; she complied with the couple's request. Self-awareness grew within me as Summer pointed to the bag. She had to register with the store and work with three different employees to complete the purchase. A man in a pressed black suit stood next to me, speaking into his wrist like James Bond.

He mumbled something in French, which I am sure meant, "Niner, niner, do you copy, we've got a code red. Two

American punks are not rich enough to be in this store, I repeat, two American punks are not rich enough to be in this store!"

Time was crawling, and I felt like we were on the wrong side of a sting operation. We left the store, handed the designer items to the Asian couple, and exchanged glances of excited dismay. Perhaps we had just aided in a sweatshop knock-off operation. Perhaps eight-year-old children would mimic the Louis Vitton item for two cents an hour. The moral depravity of it all floated away as we strolled to our next destination, Rue Cler.

Rue Cler was a pedestrian-only, cobblestone masterpiece. It was a street famous for its specialty shops. We went to different patrons for wine, cheese, pastries, and chocolate in order to assemble a gourmet picnic to eat upon the Eiffel tower.

Jean, who ran our favorite fruit-stand, humored me as I dictated my order to him, "I would like to buy two apples. Do you like apples?"

"Oui," he replied with a contagious smile.

"My sister is an apple. She calls herself Rachel. Do you come to school by autobus?" I said, in an attempt to prolong our conversation. There is a great possibility that I also asked Jean if I could use the hall pass to go to the bathroom.

The evening was chilly. We watched our exhales bubble into thick clouds as we ascended to the second balcony of the Eiffel Tower. Our picnic was perfect—a testament to the underrated beauty of being twenty-three and single in the world. The sun began to set the in March sky, and I felt intoxicated by the moment.

Chelsea met us at the hostel on a Tuesday, a day we would spend at the Palace of Versailles. The palace was immaculate, to say the least. Every detail had been embellished to such a degree that it almost made me sick. Like an ancient episode of *MTV Cribs*, the palace boasted a vast collection of whatever was in fashion during the days of Louis the Fourteenth. If the pompous ruler were alive today, I think that he'd drive a BMW with twenty-inch spinning rims and surround himself with girls from rap videos.

The three of us walked the grounds where royal men used to gather for hunting and seducing their mistresses (and each other). Fountains decorated by sea creatures and mermaids stood at the center of miles of garden pathways.

"I would love to wear the gowns from this time period," Summer said.

"Oh yeah, me too," Chelsea agreed. "They were so flattering to a lady's figure."

Like silly kids we began to waltz around a concrete fountain, pretending to be ladies in the court. We imagined our favorite activities and meals and came up with a menu and schedule to manufacture our perfect day at court.

"Breakfast with scones and coffee, and high tea with girlfriends." Chelsea suggested.

"A brisk walk with a sincere man," I said.

"A piano lesson and dancing with my friends," Summer added.

"Painting and belly dancing." Chelsea said.

"I don't think belly dancing existed." I laughed.

"Well," Summer interrupted, "maybe this list shouldn't be a fantasy. These are the little things that make us smile right now. We could have lives like this if we wanted to."

"That's true," I said.

In light of that discovery, we decided to make google-eyes at the local pastry shop and enjoy whatever we wanted, just because. Like all pastry shops in Paris, this one had desserts that were so picturesque that they could have been framed and large baguettes that children would carry home for supper. If it were possible, I'd have a Parisian pastry display counter installed in my kitchen.

Chelsea suggested that we see Paris by taking a night bike tour. It was a good way to learn about all the major monuments in a few hours. After another visit to our neighborhood pastry counter, we walked to a bike shop for our tour, and that's when I met Adam.

Adam was a Californian who took a job leading bike tours in Paris for nine months. The first thing I noticed about him was his smile. He had bright, straight teeth and smiled often, telling me that he did not take himself too seriously. His brown sculpted hair matched his glasses and gave him an adventurous vibe. He was sweet. So sweet, in fact, that Summer nicknamed him "sweet Adam." Before we started riding, Adam gave us some pointers.

"Sometimes the people in cars will honk at us. That's their way of saying 'way to go, guys, keep riding,'" he explained. "And sometimes they'll also wave their middle finger at us, that's French for 'bike tours are number one.'"

"Okay," another rider said, "but what if they moon us?"

"That's another French custom," Adam replied. "They are just trying to show you how tight your gluts are getting from all of the peddling. Now come on, let's see some stuff!"

On the bike tour we had a chance to see the Notre Dame at night. When lit up, the Notre Dame looks like three separate churches. It took so long to construct that three architectural styles influenced builders of different generations. From the front, it stands with dignified strength. From the side it frightens passersby with its creepy gargoyles. From the back, the Notre Dame invites locals into a gothic house of worship. The inside, though once used to house cattle, smells like honey because tourists and Catholics alike light hundreds of candles each day, sending prayers up to heaven.

"Famous French thinkers," Adam explained, "believed that cities should be made for people to enjoy, and built around the needs of pedestrians, instead of being built around the needs of businesses."

"I think I agree with that," I responded.

"You might not believe this, but Paris actually has more gardeners than police officers," he said.

Wow, I thought to myself.

As Adam pointed out the many grand monuments of Paris, I was saddened that we in the United States did not take the same pride in the aesthetics of our cities. Paris was very well designed. When you are on a Parisian street, you want to be romantic.

"I feel like I am in love when I walk around here. It's ro-tic," Summer said.

"Pardon me," Chelsea asked. "Ro-tic?"

"You know, romantic, without the man," Summer explained.

"Oh right, ro-tic. Well, girls," Chelsea said, "I am so glad we did this. I am thoroughly enjoying my ro-tic evening. I can't believe I am in the Northern Hemisphere with you lovely ladies."

Chelsea often said, "I am so glad we did this." It was a phrase that confirmed how much she liked us, and I made a decision to use it in the future.

"I am really curious about that building, Adam. What is it?" I asked, although, truth be told, I was really more curious about him.

"That's Ecole Militaire. Napoleon went to school there," he explained.

"Ah ha, the poster-child for short man's syndrome," I said.

"You got it, Crystal," he responded with a grin.

At the end of our tour, the three of us lingered a little bit. Girls can do that to make themselves available to guys. (It is a kind of tactic). It worked because after a few minutes Adam came up to talk to us privately.

"That was a really great tour," I said.

"Thanks. You guys were a good group. I never know what to expect with this job," he said.

There was a moment of silence and it felt like the end of a first date.

"Well," Adam said, reaching into his pocket, "here's my cell phone number—we should all hang out before you leave Paris."

"That would be great," I replied.

We would rendezvous the next night.

After spending too much time at the Louvre, we were running late for our date with Adam. For some reason, we got it in our heads that we could make better time if we took a shortcut to the Eiffel Tower—this proved false because every monument in Paris was surrounded by six feeder streets that extended to form uneven blocks. We hustled around corners only to be met with dead ends. At least the buildings gave us something to look at while we rushed around. They were constructed with broad golden-white bricks and accessorized with wrought iron balconies. Each window was impeccably dressed in long drapes. It seemed that everywhere I looked, Paris offered something beautiful.

Eventually we met Adam—we were twenty minutes late. Being late is one of my pet peeves. If you are two minutes late, it can be forgiven, but anything more than eleven minutes is just plain rude. With a gracious smile, Adam overlooked the flaw and led us on an amusing wander through the Latin Quarter. We climbed a stairwell to the top of a church tower and watched people dine from the sidewalk.

Adam unapologetically examined one group and said, "Fiery old men make the best hand gestures."

"You can't just look in the window like that!" Chelsea exclaimed.

"No, it's okay," Adam explained. "Everyone people-watches in Paris. It's part of the café culture. Go ahead, give it a try."

We peered into the window and invented words for the customers. It was like we were dubbing their conversations to English.

The next stop was a fancy dessert shop on the Isle de Cite. A banana split cost nearly ten dollars.

Summer motivated us to split desserts. "Come on, when is the next time we'll be in such a romantic place?"

"Don't you mean a 'ro-tic' place?" Chelsea corrected.

"Well, we have a man with us, right, Adam?" Summer said.

"That's right. Hey, what's that behind you guys?" Adam said, as he stole the complimentary chocolates on our place settings.

With that, the four of us had dessert and spent three hours telling funny stories. Adam grew up on a farm and told stories about birthing sheep and harvesting grapes.

"One time my dad actually called me out of school because he needed me to help pluck some chickens," he said.

"You've plucked a chicken?" I asked, in disbelief.

"Oh yeah, and that is the stinkiest thing you can imagine," he said and proceeded to tell us how to pluck a chicken.

He spoke with excitement and had all of us in hysterics. It was cute the way he tried to stifle his own laughter when telling a joke. When our desserts were gone, we ate sugar cubes and fizzy candy that Chelsea had in her purse. We had giggled away the night, and, at 1:30 a.m., missed our hostel curfew, so Adam let us sleep on the floor of his tiny apartment.

Once we all settled down in the apartment, Chelsea, in her proper Adelaide Australian accent whispered, "Do you smell something burning?"

"Yeah," said Summer.

"It's my hay-a!" Chelsea screamed.

Apparently, in our quest to fit on the floor, Chelsea had let her hair get to close to the heater. We frantically scrambled for new positions, and this time, Adam had turned his body around so that I could share his pillow. He gave up all of his blankets for us, and just when things were quiet again, Summer darted up.

"I feel sick," she exclaimed, and jetted off to the bathroom to vomit.

My heart went out to Summer because the apartment was so miniature, that we could all hear each eruption quite clearly. She blamed it on the fizzy candy, but I think it had something to do with sore abdominal muscles, as we had all been howling for hours. It was a crazy night, one that I will never forget. Adam tucked me in again, and I fell asleep with the scent of his minty exhale on the pillow next to me.

I was still thinking about Adam when we boarded a train to Chamonix, a town in the French Alps. He was so interesting, so cool. If only I had met him back in Portland, then we would have had a sufficient time period to get to know each other. Getting closer to him was out of my grasp, as my best communication option was email—cold, impersonal email. With a sigh of defeat, I leaned on the train's window, hoping that the French countryside would mend my frustration.

Chelsea and Summer were singing songs about mountains, as peaks grew taller before our very eyes. Several people had recommended that we pay a visit to Chamonix, France, and rightly so. When we stepped off of the train, the appeal of this alpine village was so strong that we immediately decided to spend an entire week there, thwarting our former plans to spend several days in Switzerland. The ambiance was spectacular. Chamonix was a vacation destination for rich Europeans, and it was almost entirely owned and run by British people (a fact that would later get me into trouble). Cobblestone streets lined ski shops and cafés where snowboarders would dine after a hard day's work. Primped-up dogs waged their tails and pranced with a style that turned me into a dog person. Columns of steep, snowy mountains that surrounded the town often provoked me into a staring contest. The graceful strength of the Alps would catch my eye until I would forget where I was, what I was doing, and even who I was.

We checked into our hostel at 5:00 p.m., just in time for half-priced beer. The three of us were seated at an outside table, watching the sunset, when we noticed something very compelling about Chamonix.

"Did anyone else notice," Chelsea began, "that the guy to girl ratio is overwhelmingly in our favor?"

"And not just that," Summer added. "All of the guys are young hot snowboarders!"

Pheromones gushed into the air, and that's when I noticed Marcus.

He was the bartender at our hostel. The moment he caught my glance, I could not stop watching him. Even the way he wiped down a table left me speechless. He had green eyes, straight eyebrows, a perfectly shaped man-nose, and (be still my heart) an English accent. My unwavering gawking was embarrassing.

"Stop it!" I scolded myself. "What if he notices you looking at him?" It was no use, my eyes had surrendered to the English snowboarder, and they were no longer taking orders from my brain.

There must be a certain hypnotic pattern in which English men speak that sucks the wit right out of me, because it took me a hour to conceive a way to meet Marcus.

"Can I borrow your hat tomorrow?" I asked.

"Yeah, sure," he replied without hesitation.

"You see," I explained, "it's Saint Patrick's day tomorrow, and I don't have anything green to wear, and since your hat is green I thought ..."

"Right, you don't want anyone to pinch you tomorrow for not wearing green," he said, catching my logic.

"Yeah," I said, and then without any permission from my brain, my mouth volunteered, "but I would pinch you."

My brain was obviously having a tough time giving orders since Marcus had come along. He smiled and winked at me. My ears burned. For once in my life I had nothing to say. All I could do was go back to my room and, in a light-headed frenzy, put on red lipstick.

Summer was, at that moment, having a similar experience. She had spent an hour laughing with Aaron, a snowboarder from New Zealand. Aaron could come up with the perfect way to make fun of anything. He was, at his core, sweet and sincere, but concealed any softness with a bad-boy edge. Summer explained to me that in a very short time, they had exchanged sad breakup stories—he even knew about Sam. At first, I was alarmed at their rapid rate of disclosure, but she assured me that he was genuine and self-confident, and any personal details they shared were treated in a strictly informational manor. We finished getting ready and joined a lively group of backpackers for a long night of fun.

Marcus and I had such an attraction that when we were next to each other, the room could have exploded. We loved the same things—France, our nieces, and politics. He had every right to be a cocky ladies man—he was terribly cute, educated, well traveled, and, by his proper carriage, I could tell that he came from money. He wasn't arrogant, though. In fact, he restrained making fast moves on me, preferring to sit with his arm holding mine while we talked about his life in Chamonix.

"Can I ask you a question?" I asked.

"You just have," Marcus replied with his quick English wit.

"Fair enough," I laughed. "So why do you live here?"

"Well, I speak French and I love snowboarding," he said. "But it's not permanent. In the next year I'll probably go back to England so that I can see my big brother. He just had a kid, kind of a surprise."

"That happened to my sister," I said. "But her daughter, Sasha, just has my heart, you know? She makes me laugh all of the time."

"Yeah. I fancy being an uncle," he said. "So after the backpacking trip, what then?"

"The tentative plan is to finish graduate school," I said. "And in the meantime journal, draw, explore."

"Tentative plan, I like that, that's good," he laughed. "So what do you draw?"

"I could draw you," I told him.

We chatted until five in the morning about all kinds of things. One of the sweetest topics still makes me smile.

"It's funny," he admitted. "The only other Crystal I knew had ginger hair like you. She was in grammar school with me, and I had a big crush on her."

"It was me!" I replied, and we both chuckled.

Smiles remained on our faces as our laughter died down. This was the first silence of the night. We moved closer to each other until I felt his lips touch mine. He held me tight, and kissed me lightly, sometimes just letting his lips rest on mine. At that moment, I didn't care that it was so late. Marcus and I stood in the cold, kissing like I've never kissed before. I could have stayed with him for hours. To this day, the English kiss is still the best I've ever experienced.

The high from kissing Marcus stayed with me the next day when Summer and I went snowboarding. This was our first try, and every few minutes we would find on ourselves a new bruise. When her New Zealander friend, Aaron, heard we were having trouble, he descended to the bunny hill to offer us a free lesson. While he taught us stops and turns, Aaron would grab Summer for a quick hug. He treated her like a precious girlfriend, and she felt special the whole day.

"Crystal," she said with a peaceful shock, "this was the anniversary of the day Sam proposed to me. And I haven't felt sad all day long."

Aaron had taken her mind away from anything sad, and I was elated for my best friend.

That evening, I walked into the hostel, and a few of Marcus' friends gave him a little nod and grin.

"How about that drawing, then?" he asked me.

"What?" I said.

"Last night you said you'd draw me," he reminded me.

He was happy to see me, and remembered all sorts of things we had discussed the night before—he must have been thinking about our conversation all day.

"Yeah, I'll draw you sometime," I said, and spent the rest of the evening in close proximity to him, chatting with Chelsea and Summer while he worked.

"Marcus," I said as he stood in front of me, only the bar between us.

"Yes, do you want some drinks or something?" he asked.

"No, I'm a good girl," I told him

"Now I don't believe that," he said, pouring a beer with one hand while giving someone change with the other.

"Yes I am!" I said, though I was not offended, just content that he was talking to me while he was so busy.

Throughout the week, Marcus offered selfless gestures of affection. He would make me coffee, greet me with a big smile and sometimes a kiss on the cheek, and he even arranged for Summer, Chelsea, and I to move into the best room in the entire hostel.

In the evenings our hostel became a makeshift family. A British-Italian man often prepared dinners while Randy, a Scot with the harshest accent I'd ever heard, cracked jokes. Summer played waitress to three Polish tourists who added extra attentive cheer. The atmosphere was so tightly knit that I never wanted to say goodbye.

My only consolation was high above the Alps. The three of us took the Aguille du Midi cable car to the highest viewpoint in the Alps—Mount Blanc. The air was clear and thin and I could see France, Italy, and Switzerland, depending on my direction. Even though I had been living in mountainous Oregon, the majesty of Mount Blanc left me breathless. Chamonix was a dream world. We had interesting characters to watch and cool guys to impress. Just like a thirteen-year-old, I imagined myself moving to Chamonix, getting one of those exquisite dogs, and living happily ever after with Marcus, the English gentleman.

Unfortunately, Marcus was such a gentleman, that I had trouble reading him. As I was later informed by several reliable English girls, when guys are raised in an upperclass home, they have too much pride (or fear) to be overtly affectionate. Had I known this at the time, I would have understood that when he made an effort to sit next to me, he was practically screaming to the world, "I really like this redhead!" However, in my west-coast American culture, I had been used to guys rolling down the windows of their Honda Civics, blasting "Baby Got Back," and shouting at me in the form of vulgar come-ons. In America, women can be shy because the men lack inhibition. In England, sadly, it is the opposite.

To this day, I wish that I had understood English culture that March. I took Marcus' restraint as a signal that he didn't like me, when it was just the way he treated the girls that he liked. He would speak freely to uncomely girls, but when I was near him, he became nervous. On one such occasion, my head boiled when he spoke with a plain tomboyish girl at the hostel. Summer, Chelsea, and I had ordered a big meal after a day of hiking, but I wanted him to approach me so badly that I couldn't even eat. It was war.

Like a jealous girlfriend, I went and changed into my best outfit and burst back into the room. Eight guys simultaneously howled at me, but I didn't care. Marcus might as well have been the only person there. In my logic, he was supposed to be the hunter, and I was supposed to wait for him. When I wanted to express my interest, I did it in the form of self-beautification. This backfired because the hotter I looked, the quieter he became until our week's stay was up. I could feel myself missing him, but left without offering any contact information. Summer and I made plans to meet up with Chelsea in Venice, and headed to Zurich, Switzerland.

The only reason we were in Zurich was because Summer's mom, Elizabeth, was meeting us the next day. (Elizabeth would join our travels for two weeks.) There was probably a lot to do in the large, Swiss city, but we didn't care. The only appealing activity for us was to sulk for hours over Starbucks coffee, reminiscing about the details of our lives in Chamonix.

"I wish I didn't miss Marcus," I said.

"Well," Summer replied, "romance means letting someone in enough to miss them when they're gone. And maybe, the ability to be that vulnerable is the most beautiful thing about romance."

Suspended by that advice, I couldn't help but think of what these little relationships did to our travel plans. We couldn't afford to spend two days a week crying in Starbucks, and that is, inevitably, where we'd end up if English men continued to find me. Still, I was proud of myself for being vulnerable. It was a skill that I'd confused as a weakness for too long.

"You know who I don't miss?" Summer said, confused by her own revelation. "Sam … I almost married Sam and right now all I can think about is Aaron and Chamonix."

The town pierced our souls—even today I still die a little bit when I hear certain songs from our time in Chamonix. We held a grudge against Zurich because it was raining, and because it lacked Aaron and Marcus.

"I'd drop everything to have one more chance with Marcus," I told Summer, not realizing that those feelings would linger to this day.

She understood. We hated Switzerland and took a train to Venice as soon as Elizabeth had arrived.

italy

The sun rose over northern Italy, leaving orange shimmer over every drop of resting water. There were vineyards stretching to houses, stretching to high hills. The Italian flag waved, welcoming me into a land of heart and home. A red ball lifted higher in the sky as a buttery croissant filled my mouth. An oncoming train rested next to mine—its clientele were businessmen with shiny heads and crisp newspapers.

While my eyes were shut, the signs changed from French to something with more gusto—something I only understood by cartoon accompaniment—Italian. Italy, for me, had meant tomato sauce and men in sports cars with bad style. I wondered if that would change. One theory I'd carried is that you could count on the areas by the train tracks to be the worst part of a place. If that were true, I figured that central Venice must be enchanting because I wanted to hug the pink and yellow buildings across from me. The grass resembled a pillow and the air a soft blanket, and if I stepped off the train, I imagined that I'd be warm.

That afternoon we met up again with Chelsea, who, to our surprise, had taken one of Summer's beauty secrets to an extreme—Chelsea had not washed her hair for two weeks. Summer has a way with advice. She will read a book, for instance, about vegetarianism and then suggest the dietary habit to her friends, neglecting to put down a cheeseburger herself. Summer was pleasantly flabbergasted at Chelsea's new hair regimen, when she realized her hypocrisy.

"I'm a hair-washing carnivore!" she cried.

We all chuckled with forgiveness. After all, if it weren't for Summer's Italian, none of us would be able to order cappuccino in Italy, and cappuccino in Italy was paradise. A perfect dollop of foam invited us to suck into a potent shot of espresso. Chelsea opted for a biscotti as well, and I was gratified to nibble on the olive bread that Summer had ordered from a curious bread shop for only fifty cents. Just then Chelsea's cell phone rang.

"Hi, David," she said.

Summer and I looked at each other in a wordless conversation while Chelsea spoke to David.

"I've got to go, this is costing me a fortune," Chelsea said. "No … I can't say it, I'm with my friends … alright … I love you too. I miss you too. Yes, I will. Okay, goodbye, David."

"He did it again, huh?" Summer said to Chelsea.

"Yes," Chelsea said. "I hate him for doing this all of the time, calling me, you know … but I love him … because he is David."

"You can't help who you love," I told Chelsea.

"No, but you can help what you do about it," said Summer. "Come on, let's go see Venice! Let's get your mind out of Australia and into Italy!"

We left to find the beauty of Italy. Venice had few grand

monuments, but rather the entire city was a sight to behold, and Elizabeth invented a new way to explore it.

The best way to see Venice is to pick an interesting looking Italian and trail behind them at a comfortable distance. The key in this kind of tour is in the choosing. You are assured a successful trail if you pick a person on a cell phone, walking with purpose. This is probably a real local on his way to work or lunch.

The four of us joyfully participated in a round of kindly stalking. We were led into all kinds of interesting Venetian streets while following a chatty group of women or an old man with groceries. Behind every corner in Venice was a hidden treasure—a pick-up soccer game, a garden, or a canal with a singing gondolier. After getting caught by a paranoid student, who insisted upon looking behind himself every two minutes, it was time to find some dinner.

We ordered a meal near San Marco Square—the most famous piazza in Italy. Portions were small. To my disappointment the spaghetti marinara on my plate would have passed for a child's portion in the United States. Perhaps that says something about the childhood obesity epidemic. In any event this is what I should have expected because, according to Summer, Italians did not order pasta for a main dish, but rather, fish. To expect pasta for a main course was as American as speaking at a painfully high decibel while adjusting one's WWF tee shirt. Since we had followed locals around for miles, I was starving, and attempted to stretch my meal with spoonfuls of Parmesan cheese. Our waiter noticed my gluttonous cheese consumption and, shaking his head, scolded me in Italian. My shoulders sunk in shame. It was a good thing that I could not understand Italian.

On the way home we had to abandon all navigational logic and walk over bridges until we reached the Ferrovia (the train station) to get to our hotel. A group of guys saw us and started chanting, *"Bacio, bacio"* (kiss). A pleasantly tipsy young man wore a wreath around his neck and a bottle in his hand. Apparently he was having his bachelor party and he had to kiss any girl the group shouted at. He cornered me until I kissed his cheek. In the United States, someone might be arrested for accosting a group of girls while intoxicated, which begs the question—is it really still the land of the free?

After saying a final goodbye to Chelsea, we headed southward to Rome. Since Summer had been to Rome before, she contrived for us an incredible walking tour that took us to Trevy Fountain, the Trestavere district, the Pantheon, and the Spanish Steps. Young people on the steps drank bottles of wine in the open air, happy to just be together. Dozens of strangers sung along to a melodious guitar that crossed every language barrier. I walked to the top of the steps by myself to find adjectives that described Rome. With a group of palm trees waving at me, I decided that Rome was clean, tropical, antiquated, solid, whimsical, and influential.

The next day, we sat in a café outside of the Coliseum. The structure was an anachronism. It stood tall, still bragging about the times when animals pounced at gladiators whose fate was either through the door of life or the door of death. The very ground on which I stood was once home to men like Julius Caesar and Apostle Paul. As a reminder of that, our tour guide had the profile of a Roman sculpture. We listened as he told us the great secrets of the Coliseum.

"Often the animals were starved for seven days before these matches so that in their hunger, they would tear the gladiators to shreds," he said, giving us a graphic image that lasted into the afternoon.

Elizabeth was making good use of her new digital camera at the Coliseum. She took photos of the ruins at various angles, and we all enjoyed the instant gratification of seeing her pictures. One of the shots was a close-up of me.

"Wow, Crystal," she remarked, "you have such a beautiful smile."

"Really?" I questioned.

I was not fishing for any additional compliments, but rather I was truly perplexed. My entire life, I had been convinced that I should hide my smile. In group photos, my friends joke that I always have a corny pose and expression. What my friends do not know is that this is intentional. If I were to smile for real, everyone could see my short, square teeth. To the untrained eye, my teeth look straight enough, but I know that one incisor sticks out a bit. Also, when I smile, my cheeks squish upward like a child and my eyes disappear into tiny slits.

Elizabeth made a point to find several photos that she had saved in her camera to zoom in on my smile. She politely forced me examine the photos for myself.

"See, Crystal, you have a really cute smile, and you should show it more often," she said.

Smiling makes other people feel good. It is something I can give away, it doesn't cost a thing, and it is worth so much. A smile tells someone that they are accepted and cared for—a message that my inhibitions had, thus far, prevented me from expressing. It took Italy to convince me that I had a nice smile. An expensive lesson, for such an inexpensive gesture.

We spent our last days with Elizabeth in Florence, trapped on a tourist highway. Tired students and pickpockets pushed their way around us as a dozen gelato stands shouted for our patronage. Souvenir kiosks spat out Florentine junk of every variety. You could purchase anything with a statue of David on it—with or without a leaf censoring his anatomy. If Michelangelo were alive today, I wondered if he would sport his work on a wife-beater tank top. Would the artist, like the Midwestern tourists behind me, overlook the fact that the threading in his tank top was coming undone with every twist of his torso? Maybe. Then again, on the tourist highway, when accompanied by white sneakers and fanny packs, such fashion violations seemed minor.

At the Duomo in Florence, pigeons outnumbered people. I have never understood why people enjoy playing with pigeons. To me, they are rats that fly. They peck around without proper fear of the fact that I am 75 times their size, and pester me so that I cannot enjoy the outdoors. Pigeons have horrible social boundaries and often carry lice and bacteria. When you don't feed them, even when you kick at them, they return within minutes, forgetting that they are completely unwelcome. Pigeons are the annoying younger cousins of the bird family.

We stood in front of the Duomo, an antiquated structure polluted by car exhaust, and though we tried to appreciate its beauty, at best the three of us could only relate to its battered state. After walking all day and playing the rope in a tug of war between tourist shops, the four of us (Elizabeth, Summer, the Duomo, and I) were exhausted. We escaped, slipping onto a forgotten back street, and that was where Florence became beautiful.

Our only company came in the form of two local mini-mart owners. Their stores faced each other, and somehow forgot that they were in competition. The owners stood outside, arguing about something passionately with smiles on their faces and laughter on their breath. They were delighted to help three ladies pick out foreign candy, and we were delighted to have the help. So helpful, they were, in fact, that we asked them for a cheap-yet-delicious-restaurant recommendation. The men sent us down the street to a friend's little diner, a place I'll never forget.

The restaurant had five tables. Jugs of red wine were pre-poured and the staff memorized everyone's order. This was the local piece of culinary heaven I had always imagined. As opposed to the restaurants near all the tourist traps, this place was really affordable, and since it was Elizabeth's last evening with us, we felt compelled to order whatever we wanted. We would have an appetizer, a salad, a pasta, a wine, and a dessert. We might have to be rolled out of the joint in a few hours, but that caused in us no hesitation.

One of the key phrases I learned in Italian was: "I am a vegetarian, is this one okay?" (accompanied by my pointing at the menu). This is how I ordered a five-course meal. Summer did not share my dietary restrictions, and proceeded to simply point away at whatever looked interesting. The evening was filled with mystery. For one, it was an enigma what sex the server actually was. He/she spoke in a low for a girl, but high for a man's voice. He/she had short, slicked hair and a baggy white dress shirt. Fortunately, if we called him/her with the wrong word, the language barrier was our scapegoat. Another mystery appeared when the ambiguously-gendered person set before Summer her first coarse. Summer did her best to poke around the meat substance, not recalling, at that moment, the correct words for various farm animals. When she couldn't feign her disgust any longer, Summer called him/her over to our table.

"What kind of meat is this?" Summer asked.

He/she wasn't offended in the least. Rather professionally,

our server proceeded to pantomime a chicken. If I were playing charades, I would definitely pick him/her to be on my team. He/she was focused at the task at hand and within seconds, we all realized that Summer had been eating chicken liver.

"Eew!" Summer said, catching the attention of another table.

Luckily, the other courses consisted of normal and delicious ingredients.

As we enjoyed the rest of our meal, it became apparent that this cozy hole in the wall was a local secret. People began to show up one after another—and it was only a Tuesday night. As the line for a spot at one of the coveted five tables wound around the restaurant, and eventually around the block, I began to feel a twinge of guilt that we had ordered so many courses.

"Nonsense," Elizabeth reasoned. "We may be tourists, but we have every right to enjoy this place. Besides, we were sent here by a local."

And with that, we slowly sipped espresso and let fluffy pieces of tiramisu make their way around our tongues.

Just as expected, I was stuffed beyond recognition. If it weren't for the fresh night air tapping at my cheeks, I would probably have gone into a starch coma. The stars gave off a hazy twinkle, and with each step violin music grew louder, until we reached its source. This was no ordinary violin music. The player was a wiry Indian-Italian boy who held his instrument incorrectly while casually sucking on a cigarette. His bow slid forcefully across the four strings, stopping everyone on the street. This was the best violinist I had ever heard. He would close his eyes and feel the music. We could all feel it as well. When he finished a legato piece, we all craved another legato. If he started a waltz, it was the only song anyone wanted to hear. Vivaldi, Mozart, and Beethoven—all became our favorite artist, depending on whom he was playing at the time. A dozen songs passed and a sizeable crowd gathered until we realized that we had been sitting on cold concrete for an hour. His violin case was open for donations in the form of change, but this adolescent prodigy was worth bills. One day, I predicted, he would be a world-class composer.

Contented, we made our way back to our room. My eyes sank into sleep, relishing the thought that I had just experienced an evening of Tuscan perfection.

After Elizabeth left, we stayed with Summer's Italian relatives. In only four days, I had gone from speaking absolutely no Italian, to understanding most conversations, and contributing the fifteen phrases that I did speak. Never in my life did I think I would understand Italian. In these provincial homes, our days were full of *bacio* on each cheek and brown-haired people pushing food our way and saying "*Mangia, mangia*" (eat more). Trying to be helpful, one of them accidentally ripped the handle off of my backpack, but I quickly forgave him because of his eager cordiality.

The family took us to beautiful Mediterranean towns, a stone's throw from Sicily. It actually felt like I could have thrown a stone over there. We had a traditional three-hour lunch in a town that was so medieval, cars couldn't fit on its streets, so we had to approach it by foot. Summer's family was very generous. If we even mentioned something that we liked, they would lavish it on us many times over. In less than a week, I became a walking ball of chocolate and cannolis.

In one household, generations of family and friends gathered to share pizza that was made in an industrial-sized oven in the backyard. After feasting on such toppings as cheese with red pepper and potato with rosemary, everyone congregated in the basement to sing karaoke. No one was embarrassed to sing, besides Summer and me. We listened to a vocal variety showcase where the ten-year-olds danced with the twenty-year-olds, who hummed along with the fifty-year-olds. The family was very close. Our evening closed with Summer's cousin, Phillipo, bellowing out "When the Saints Go Marching In," in the soulful style of a southern gospel band. Phillipo might not have known what he was singing, but Summer did, and it touched her deeply.

Before we went to sleep, Summer admitted, "When I was a kid, I was always jealous of families like this. I always wanted to have a big family that got along and had fun together."

"Is that part of the reason you didn't marry Sam, because you fought too much?" I responded.

"Well, yeah, but watching the singing tonight I realized something," she said. "This is my family."

For the rest of our time in Italy, Summer observed the little quirks about her family that she liked. Some of her cousins were very stylish—the kind of stylish that is even risky. Sophia, age 21, had a haircut similar to Pat Benetar, and somehow could pull it off. The mullet was a hairstyle that we thought would never be resurrected, and yet, when accompanied by designer jeans, it fit Sophia. Claudia had a lot of reason to be arrogant—she had just finished a rigorous university program in Rome, but instead she was humble and beamed at everyone. Patricio, at age six, had lost his father, and despite speaking very little, he still had the inner resolve to smile when he saw his father's photograph. These people were treasures, and even though our language barrier was a strain, we willingly participated in pantomiming and *bacio* to bridge the gap.

Bacio was a skill that gave both Summer and I a bit of

trouble. My sharp cheekbones often cause injury to these strangers. Whenever we saw family, even if there were fifteen people, we had to kiss them on each cheek. The *bacio* was actually more of a cheek tap than a kiss, and had I known that from the start, maybe I wouldn't have clonked heads so many times. By the end of Italy, the tenderhearted locals needed a break from the splitting headaches I was giving them. At least that's what I figured as Summer and I boarded a train to the Adriatic, where we'd take a ferry to Greece.

greece

Summer and I knew that going all the way to Greece was a long journey. What we did not know was just how many appalling positions we would confront on the voyage. On a train from Bologna to the Italian coast, we were ushered out of a first-class cabin, thrown to the dogs, as we searched for another seating arrangement. In one cabin, middle-aged Italian snobs smoked us away. They lit cigarettes until my clothes smelled like a bingo hall and were stiff with tar. Summer fell into a fit of coughing and the ladies rolled their eyes with egotistical apathy. Our search continued. After being thrown out of the dining car, we resorted to sitting in a luggage compartment, or what may have previously been a toilet. There was stiff hay pointing at my rear and first-class passengers eyed us with contempt.

"I need to put my suitcase down, and you are blocking the luggage compartment." A snooty passenger told me.

"I think there is room on that shelf," I said.

"Well, there are bags in the way," she said, insisting that I find a place for her gigantic suitcase.

Reluctantly, I rearranged some bags for the woman, bruising my leg in the process. All I wanted to do was sleep, but this was not possible, as my only pillow was the vinyl wall behind me. Summer and I had spent a lot of money to secure train transport, and we were treated like second-class citizens.

Our troubles did not flee when we boarded the ferry. Dozens of Greek men with uni-brows and gold chains stared as if we were on display. Was this the first time they had ever seen a redhead? As a western girl, I had to fight the urge to assume that I was being objectified. As usual, Summer would try and make polite eye contact with the other passengers, smiling and even saying hello.

"Hi," Summer said to a man in a uniform.

"Hello," he responded. "Your first time in Greece?"

"Not my first time," Summer said. "Do you work on the boat?"

"Yes," he answered proudly, and then attempted to make further conversation.

After he left, we sat on a pink bench, writing in our journals. A few minutes later he came back.

"Hello again," Summer said.

"Would you girls like to come back to my room?" he asked us.

Incredible. We couldn't even have an innocent conversation without being propositioned. Had these people no respect for women? Maybe east of the Adriatic, women spent more time looking at the floor than the sky, and we had to take on that custom as well. In mortification, I began to hang my head to evade the uncomfortable staring we were receiving.

My shame melted away on the top deck of the boat, somewhere between Greece and Italy. The ocean was grape and the sky was amber. We were on the open sea with the best view possible and Greek and Italian occasionally on the loudspeaker. Summer and I had been leisurely watching the sun melt into the ocean and dreaming about guys. Life was good. Dusk created a pink that could not be mimicked by Crayola. All I heard was the dance of wind on waves—forceful and peaceful. This place had been breathing for ages, long before I sipped my first breath, and I had the privilege to be a part of it. The sway of the boat transported me to a place of blissful reflection.

The rocking did not, unfortunately, have the same effect on Summer. In the middle of the night, she shot up in a manner that reminded me of our time in Paris. We would relive that moment at Adam's apartment. She ran to a couple of bathrooms, knowing that she only had thirty seconds to find one that was unlocked—no such luck. Summer collapsed back on the bench where we were camping and threw her head into a plastic bag. Not since the movie *Stand by Me* had I seen such an exorbitant display of vomiting.

It was a sunny day and the white sand glowed, begging to be marched over. The Ionian Sea, I decided, was the prototype that artists used to make the color turquoise. Brown cliffs stood over the ocean like a concerned older brother. The pathway to our hotel was lined with lavender, which emitted a strong fragrance. The island was like a girl dressed up for a date. She wore a tropical dress, with her hair tossed above her head in easy curls. She splashed lavender perfume on her wrists so that enchanted explorers would notice her when she subtly breezed by. This was the vacation from our vacation.

We checked into our hotel to find a plump Greek girl smiling with all sorts of promises.

"You get to stay one day free," she began. "There is a

complimentary breakfast every morning and a traditional Greek meal served every night—this is also complimentary. You can rent anything that you need, including cars and kayaks, and we have lots of tours that take you around the island. Would you like to see your room?"

Would we ever! The hotel had beachfront property and more perks than we could count. We wondered if the room would be as marvelous. Indeed it was. Summer and I had our own clean bathroom and breezy balcony. Our sheets were bleached and we even had a spare bed.

In disbelief, Summer said to me, "I'm surprised there isn't some sort of catch—this is the nicest place we've stayed so far."

I agreed. After twenty-four hours of difficult travel, we were finally queens on a Greek island. We napped away our weariness until it was time for dinner.

Greek salad, baklava, and other indigenous edibles waited for us in the dining room. The anticipation in our palate was surpassed only by the anticipation of our company. We expected to meet interesting Australian backpackers or hunky Greek athletes. In this tropical place we predicted to kayak and explore with friends from around the globe. Instead, waiting for us in the dining room was a group of self-indulgent American exchange students with nothing to talk about outside of the realm of beer.

Placing my dinner on a big round table, I introduced myself to some girls from UCLA. "Hi, I'm Crystal."

"Hi," one replied. "I'm Buffy, what's your major?"

This reminded me of my freshman year of college. Whenever college freshman meet, they ask each other a list of boring questions as if they were filling out a survey. The most common are: "What's your name?" "What's your major?" "What's your minor?" "What town are you from?" And, "What sports did you play in high school?"

Humoring Buffy's surface conversation, I told her, "Mass communications, political science, Keizer, Oregon, track and cheerleading."

"Hi," another girl said to me. "My name is Ashley, and I go to the University of Florida. What's your name? What are you studying in college?"

"I'm Crystal," I responded. "Umm, mass communications."

Even though I had already graduated from college, I was sucked back into it, and only into the lame parts of it—the parts where people depended too much on course outlines and superficial relationships.

Glancing at Summer, I overheard her tell a guy from Arizona State, "I'm Summer, and I majored in business."

Everyone in the room was American and sported a college sweatshirt. The ringleader of the group was a guy named Jordan. Jordan, I decided, spent more time at the gym than at class, drank protein shakes, and probably hadn't read a book without pictures. He assessed the crowd, making a mental list of the hottest girls. Since the drinking age in Greece was much younger than in America, Jordan used alcohol to persuade half-witted girls to flash him. When he tried to talk to me I just avoided him, fearing that he might suck the intelligence right out of my brain. At midnight, the hotel turned into a free-for-all, and I felt like I was trapped on an episode of *MTV Spring Break*.

That was the catch that Summer had mentioned. The resort was no less than a compound for young Americans to drink and make fools of themselves without parental supervision. The only thing Greek about it was the salad they served at dinner, and the staff never got anything done. There were no cars to rent and it was too secluded to explore the island by foot. We were trapped at the hotel and I wondered if it was all a communal religion, run by an alcoholic evil genius. Just in case my premonitions were correct, I avoided Kool-Aid that week. On nice days, being stuck on the hotel's property was not a problem because we would suntan the hours away, listening to a sweet breeze rush through palms. However, when it rained, everyone had to sit around folding tables and create games as if on a long family road trip.

In the midst of a tropical storm, we befriended Bret and Ben, a couple of Canadians who had a million stories about bears.

"One time I was working in the forest, and this bear came up to me because she thought I was endangering her cub, and so I had to shoot her." Bret said.

Bret told many other stories shooting bears. In Canada, he carried a gun on his person, because most Canadian men seem to work in forestry and carry guns. Summer theorized that you could ask any Canadian man to tell you a story about a bear, and they would have at least twelve. One out of five would have a story about a bear playing hockey. During our week in Greece, this proved to be true. The Canadians were great company because they were also fed up with all of the vapid coeds at the compound.

"If I have to answer the question, 'Like, what are you studying in college' one more time, I might run screaming into the ocean," I said.

Everyone agreed with me. In response to this, Ben, Summer, Bret, and I compiled a list of lame answers in case someone else asked what we studied.

"Dental Hygiene and the British culture"

"Narcolepsy and dating."

"Broadcasting and the social trends of inbreeds, also known as daytime television."

"Probability in concealed experiments, also known as 'How many fingers am I holding up?'"

Sadie and Betsy, exchange students studying in Spain, joined our table and suggested that we all play cards. Sadie and Betsy had thick Wisconsin accents, and I loved to mimic them.

"They say that the Midwestern accent is the most phonetically correct way of speaking English." Sadie informed me.

"Maybe that is true, but it doesn't stop the splitting headache I get every time I go to a family reunion in Chicago," I replied in jest.

In spite of my jabs at her speech, Sadie quickly extended an invitation for Summer and I to stay with Betsy and her in Madrid. There was something different about these girls. They were confidant and funny, and offered glances of peace and hope. What kind of a person would invite us to stay after only a day? Something was up. With that thought I continued, with Ben, to add to our fabricated list of studies.

"The psychological effects of post-celebrity incarceration, also known as *E! True Hollywood Story.*"

"Electronic background music, also known as karaoke."

"Molecular botany as it pertains to dairy."

"The social ramifications of methane emission."

"Rapid eye movement and heavy machinery."

"Square dancing."

At that point the list got too stupid for even Jordan to believe. Ben and I were amused, and that was quite a feat for a rainy day at the compound.

Just then Jordan caught my glance. He was in the corner of the room, reading a book.

Jordan reads? I thought, puzzled.

"What are you reading?" I asked him.

"Greek mythology," he replied. "I am trying to read a book for every country I visit."

"That sounds cool," I responded.

Guilt entered my heart. How could I be so quick to come up with a character verdict about some kid whom I had only just met? He sat quietly, studying his book. Jordan was just a harmless guy, and I was a judgmental know-it-all.

Summer and I finally got the chance to leave the compound. We shared a taxi into town to observe the Easter traditions of Greece. One of the traditions was to throw clay pots off of balconies to remember the time the women found the empty tomb and dropped their containers of spices for Jesus' body. When we were walking through town, we had to watch where we stepped because there were shards of broken pots everywhere. Also, it was common to see a funeral procession, and they even rigged some sort of blast to recreate the time that the earth shook almost two-thousand years ago. There was no sign of an Easter bunny or chocolate eggs. Summer and I were not Greek Orthodox, but still found their zeal to be worthy of respect.

We walked along a market where families sold anything from knock-off Louis Vitton handbags to wooden spoons. A ten-year-old girl offered me a handbag, and while she was gesturing in Greek, I realized that our purchase at the Champs Elysees in Paris might have put the poor girl to work.

"That girl should be playing with dolls or jumping rope with her friends, but because of me, she is sitting in an open-air market, peddling handbags," I said.

"If she wasn't selling knock-off handbags, she'd be selling wooden spoons," Summer assured me.

"You're probably right, but I still feel bad," I said as we continued on.

Buildings in the old Greek town were painted with vibrant pastels, like yellow and salmon. It was common to see a gorgeous stairwell half-painted and half-tarnished. Buildings wore flowers on their ledges and rusty cars on their streets.

"Someone once told me," Summer recalled, "that anything is beautiful when done in repetition. Like, one of these buildings looks run down by itself, but put it in a row of twenty and it has character."

Sure enough, Summer was right. Beauty by repetition was a signature of Greece. Her theory opened my eyes to a cute house that had a shabby chicken coop in the front yard. I saw a lavender field with broken car in it. The car must have been there a while because it was growing lavender in its engine. There was also a mold-ridden wall embellished with cascading flowers. We finished the day by conversing with the locals about all of the Easter ceremonies. One shop owner flirted with Summer and recognized that we were not Greek. My red hair might have given that away.

"So," he asked, "are you staying at that resort across the Island?"

We didn't want to answer. We didn't want to be associated with that place in any way, and we were glad to leave it. In the spirit of backpacking, we would take Sadie and Betsy up on their offer, and meet them in Madrid, Spain.

spain

Summer and I made our way toward Spain, via Cannes, France. Unfortunately, we didn't see any stars there for the film festival—and too bad, because I really wanted to get Gérard Depardieu's autograph. However, the Azure Coast was home to shiny yachts, sports cars, and the lovely country of Monaco. We spent a day in the south of France, on the Isle de Saint Marguerite, the setting of Alexander Dumas' *The Man in the Iron Mask*. The island was beautiful with clear skies, salty air, and trees that smelled like camping. The water reflected the sun, dancing like a disco ball as yachts lazily swayed by, taking on the rhythm of the waves. Only the ocean spoke at that moment, telling us a story about nature and peace and harmony—melodious comfort. The temperature was perfect— warm with a tiny breeze that blew over the water's surface so that it twinkled, and I pretended that a thousand tourists were snapping our picture.

Turning to Summer, I said, "This must be the deserted island everyone refers to when they ask, 'If you could bring three things on a deserted island, what would they be?'"

"Well, what's your answer to that?" she asked.

"I guess a book, a musical instrument, and an English guy," I said.

"Orlando Bloom?" she asked.

"Actually, I was thinking about another English guy for once," I said. "Marcus."

"He's gone, Crystal," she reminded me. "Does that make you think twice about playing hard-to-get?"

Biting my lip, I admitted, "Yeah. I've got to get over this shy thing. Anyway, what's your answer, what would you bring?"

"Joe Nichols, the Bible, and Joe's guitar," she said.

That was a good answer. Summer was beginning to know what she wanted.

Heading southward, we took a night train, hoping to sleep our way to Spain. Instead we were bothered by a wild pack of French teenagers who were clearly intoxicated. They yelled at each other and kept opening our cabin door. The noise and pestering grew in volume, and we began to fear for our safety. By the time the train conductor came to check our tickets, Summer was so frenzied that she started yelling at him in Italian—for the rest of the ride, he thought that she was Italian. When I explained our safety concerns in my best French, he escorted us to first class. During all of the chaos with the hoodlums, I lost my camera. Too bad I didn't lose my backpack.

It is actually possible for a backpack to be so heavy that it makes someone tip over. And by someone, I mean me. The next day in a train station, I dropped a bunch of important papers on the floor. As I went to pick them up, the 35 pounds on my back gave way and I felt myself tipping over in slow motion. An older man reached at the air while spouting something in Spanish, which I can only imagine was a remark of concern. Momentum got the best of me and I landed like an upside down turtle. Rolling over to my knees, I picked up my papers and pressed myself up as if on a weight machine. The fall had further torn my shoddy backpack, and I couldn't wait to put it down in Sadie and Betsy's apartment. Truly the worst part of backpacking around Europe was the backpack.

The best thing about backpacking around Europe was making friends with strangers. We did not know Sadie and Betsy that well and were surprised to find that they had rearranged their room so that we would be comfortable. They knew Madrid and showed us around.

Madrid was all it was cracked up to be. A town that never slept—except for a few annoying hours in the middle of the day that forced tourists to get nothing done. When you go to Madrid, it is imperative that you change your entire schedule around. Wake up at noon, get out of the house at 2:30, hang out at Retiro Park under the sun for 3 hours, get a coffee, try to overlook the lisp you hear, shop for eighties-fabulous shirts in the Sol district, regroup with new friends for 9:30 dinner or *tapas*, get ready for the clubs, head to your first club at 12:30 or 1 a.m., go to the next one every few hours, catch the metro at 6 a.m. (because that's when it starts running again), and finally, go to sleep.

Sadie and Betsy gave us a forewarning about their eclectic roommates. Two girls were from Belgium, and preferred to pair off. Two guys were from Mexico, and loved to go dancing. One of them, Pablo, was a flaming homosexual.

"Hola!" Pablo said, as he approached me in an empty room.

His mouth hung open as he played with my hair and said, "I

just love red hair. And little dots on the skin."

"Freckles?" I asked.

"Jess, Freckles," he said and he ran his finger down my barren shoulder to look for more freckles.

Pablo was very affectionate. This, I figured, was because he wanted to be "one of the girls." He sat on a bed with me, in direct violation of my personal bubble.

"Have you ever been to the United States?" I asked him.

"Jess, my family goes to Texas for shopping," he said.

Pablo came from a rich Mexican family that would take expensive trips up to San Marcos, Texas, just to buy sneakers. When I lived in Texas, I recalled seeing fancy sport utility vehicles with Mexican license plates and women with walkie-talkies speaking Spanish to one another while browsing at fuchsia pantsuits. Pablo was familiar with Texas, and proceeded to draw and invisible map on my thigh. When he inched upward to point out Dallas, I cocked my head to the side and squinted at him. If he weren't gay, I'd swear that he was trying to seduce me.

A few minutes later, Summer, Sadie, Betsy, and I went for a stroll around Retiro Park.

"Pablo was certainly friendly when I met him today," I said to the girls.

"What are you talking about?" Betsy asked. "Pablo isn't going to be home until tomorrow."

"No, he was in your room today, Pablo, the gay one, right?" I responded.

Betsy chuckled. "No, that was Marcos. He's very straight, in fact he is juggling three girlfriends right now."

"That explains it," I said. "Today, when I met him, he had his hands all over me and even drew an invisible map on my thigh. I let him do it because I thought he was gay!"

All of us burst into laughter. Marcos might have overstepped his bounds, but he had a good heart and turned out to be quite a dancer.

Back in Portland, Summer and I decided that our trip would be the most worthwhile if, in every city, we immersed ourselves in the local culture. In Madrid, that involved dance clubs and soccer. For four nights in a row I adhered to the Madrid party schedule. Sadie had a birthday one evening, and a large group of us danced the night away at the Palacio, the coolest club in the world. It had several dance floors and we could choose to throw down some hip-hop or salsa, depending on which room we entered. Women were a hot commodity at the club, and five minutes would not go by without a spicy Spaniard approaching one of us for a dance. It was stuffy and glorious, but I needed a break

"I'm going to go to the ladies room," I told Summer and Sadie.

Shoving my way off of the dance floor, a muscular guy with dark hair grabbed my hand and pulled me to himself. His confidence and direct approach were enough to convince me to stay and dance with him for two songs. He twirled me and guided my feet to an upbeat Spanish tune and we didn't exchange a word. We couldn't. The rhythm of the music spoke for us, and after my heart had been tortured in confusion from the English gentleman, this Spaniard's unfailingly forward demeanor was refreshing. The bold treatment from my mystery dance partner was common among Spanish men. Oftentimes they would approach me to strike up a strained conversation in English.

"My English is not good," they would say, and then proceed to talk my freaking ear off.

Not long before Summer and I came to Madrid, there was a terrorist bombing on the shuttle train from Madrid to Seville. We decided to use that shuttle anyway.

"We can't let terrorism prevent us from living, and besides, security is always better right after an attack," Summer reasoned.

With that in mind, we took a day trip to Seville. Stepping off the train I was initially disappointed by the southern city. The streets were bleached from the sun and the only thing beautiful about them were the orange trees that grew freely on each corner. Knowing that we could not judge Seville simply by the areas that were close to the train station, Summer and I proceeded to the old town.

Narrow streets displayed red doors with ceramic tiles. Bright laundry dangled from balconies, and old men played chess outside of *tapas* bars. Flamenco dancers paraded in front of the main cathedral in traditional costumes. Seville was gorgeous. Summer and I toured the town on a horse-drawn buggy. Our driver was a plump, light-haired boy who periodically turned to us to point out different monuments in Spanish. We couldn't understand him, but admired his sweet effort anyway.

He was proud to have us in his buggy and said something to his coworkers in Spanish, which I think meant, "Eat your hearts out, you jealous sangria-drinking wannabes."

He took us past the most beautiful park in the world, the Maria Luisa. It had tiny benches that invited couples to sit together and read poetry. Red flowers cascaded off of these benches and enhanced the color of a hundred different trees. Every few meters, a statue or fountain stopped a local in the middle of his afternoon walk, for a few minutes of art appreciation. Outside of the park, people hunted for stylish bargains at shops that all sold the exact same pink pants. Summer and I bought a few items from a trendy clothing store, hoping that 1980s fashion would return to the United States as rampantly as it had in Spain. After all, Seville had more leg warmers per capita than any place on the planet.

We returned to Madrid for a long night of girl talk with Sadie and Betsy. The four of us shared our thoughts about guys and the future just like we were at a slumber party.

"During this trip I've realized how important good friends are," Summer said. "I miss people from home. You know, people who have known me for a long time."

Sadie, Betsy, Summer, and I loved life in Europe, but since we were all Americans, and we could relate to the same culture, we began listing all of the things we missed about home.

"Reese's peanut butter cups!" Sadie shouted.

"Men who wear deodorant!" I added.

"My niece, Ruby," Summer said. "One day I want to have a kid just like her."

"My church!" Betsy said.

That comment sparked a two-hour conversation about religion, and suddenly I realized why these Midwestern strangers were so peaceful. Betsy and Sadie were very real. They didn't put on religious airs, but instead accepted who they were and trusted that God would change them for the better.

"Most of the time," Sadie explained, "when people hear the word *Jesus*, they picture a list of rules or an angry God who sits in Heaven frowning at them."

My mind drifted to the televangelism channel where pushy women with purple hair and too much makeup scolded viewers into donating money to the we-need-more-tacky-gold-furniture-on-the-set fund.

"Most people have been hurt by religion," Sadie continued.

"What we want to do is let people know that Jesus took away all of our guilt on the cross—it is finished. We don't live our lives trying to please God with what we do, but rather we love God because of what he has done for us. God can look upon us in complete satisfaction because of what Jesus did for us."

"That sounds too easy," I argued.

"It sounds easy, but it actually isn't. Most people want to trust in their own good works to get into heaven," Sadie said. "People are control freaks and are too prideful to trust that Jesus' sacrifice was sufficient."

Religion was a touchy subject. Yet these girls handled it with tact and intelligence. We were happy to stay with them for a week, and then planned to go to Switzerland.

After a grueling day at the train station, a ticket salesperson informed me that Summer and I could not leave until the next day. Even if the girls never said it, I felt like we had overstayed our welcome, so I bought tickets for that train. Summer and I arrived at the train station with fifteen minutes to spare. As we flashed our boarding passes, a concerned attendant motioned to us that we were at the wrong train station. Like an idiot, I had not bothered to look at our tickets and see that there were two train stations in Madrid. We had to board a shuttle to the other station and sprint to try and catch our train.

During the rush, I began in inhale harder and harder. My nose sniffled and my eyes dripped. I cried for thirty minutes, right there in the train station, frustrated and unable to speak. We missed our train, lost money for the reservation, and I was not about to go back to Sadie and Betsy's apartment and further inconvenience them. Summer had to do all of the rearranging because I was defeated by my failed attempt to get us on a train to Switzerland. Luckily, there was another train in three hours. Summer handed me my new ticket and waited until I shared my frustration.

"I am so stupid," I told her. "I am sorry that I took us to the wrong station."

"It was an honest mistake, Crystal. I just don't know how to react when you stop talking like that," she said.

"That's my way of dealing with things. I internalize my feelings so that I don't explode on people," I told her.

"You don't have to hold things in all the time," she said. "I am not going to just run away if we disagree on something. Conflict is not bad, as long as you handle it maturely."

Maybe my chronic avoidance of conflict was rooted in the fear that if I did not behave perfectly, my friends would run away. Summer's commitment to be my friend even during those tense moments offered some security. I realized that within the bounds of good friendships, we grow into trusting human beings.

As we boarded our train, my backpack ripped another hole, exposing my underwear to the other people in the waiting room. Embarrassed that the entire room knew about my days-of-the-week underwear, I'd never been so happy to board a train.

switzerland

After a day of travel, we were in Switzerland. While departing our train, one of the straps on my backpack tore right off, forcing me to carry it all on one shoulder, all the way to the town of Gimmewald.

Perhaps you have never heard of Gimmewald. Don't feel stupid. This little alpine town has a population of 139 (or 138 depending if Hans died last year as suspected). To get to Gimmewald we had to take two trains, a bus, a cable car, and then a van. The little village had been there for ages, and I couldn't understand how people lived so far removed from civilization. The citizens of Gimmewald had to make special arrangements with the sole commuter van in town just to go buy groceries. Trips up and down the mountain were precious, and the van was packed beyond maximum capacity. We rode along a steep ravine with eight adults, four kids, and I think a goat or two. Every muscle in my body tightened, fearing that we'd roll off of the mountain, and I could only hope that all of the passengers piled on top of one another were not distracting the driver.

We arrived at our youth hostel to find Greta, the manager, cursing at a broken computer in German. The Swiss were sort of like Germans, only quirkier. They resembled Jim Henson characters, with mismatched hair and googly eyes. When Greta took a sick day, I imagined that Fozzy Bear or Miss Piggy might take her place. Everything in the hostel world was done under the table. Instead of job interviews, hostel owners would solicit honest-looking travelers to work in exchange for free lodging. That interested me enough, but in the end I knew that traveling around was more worthwhile than a free stay.

Almost immediately, Summer and I met Matt and Steve. Matt was a Polish-American from Chicago, who repeated the same jokes to anyone just entering the hostel. He also happened to go to the same high school as my cousins. Steve was an ex-football player from Portland, and he knew a lot of jocks who went to my high school.

"Do you know my cousin? She was in the color guard at your high school," I asked Matt.

"What year?" He asked.

"1998," I said.

"Too young," he responded.

"Well, do you know Joe Smith?" Steve asked me. "He played football at your school freshman year."

"Yeah, I think I remember that guy," I said. "What about his friend, you know, the one with the dark hair?"

"Oh, that guy," Steve said. "I was in a special league with him."

We traveled to such a remote place in the world only to spend thirty minutes playing the do-you-know-so-and-so game. Unbelievable.

The mountains were so tall that when I looked out the window, I only saw snow. They protected Gimmewald like a bouncer at a nightclub. The Alps offered sturdy tranquility, and I began to reflect upon my life. Even as a grown woman, I still felt responsible for the happiness of my parents. They were trying to work everything out and stay married—none of us knew what was best. I would survive if they were together or divorced, but I would not be able to watch my dad isolate himself into a lonely pit. Nor would I be able to see my mom crushed by unhealthy communication. I never demanded that my parents bear my emotional scars, but as their child I took theirs upon myself without question.

"I don't want my parents to be miserable," I told Summer.

"Crystal," she answered, "you have no control over that. They make their own choices."

Summer's observation resuscitated my soul, and I felt my disfigured, worried countenance lift into a smile. She was right. My parents were the only people who could improve their lives. Even with my strongest encouragement, I could not go inside of my parents and adjust their attitudes. Instead of wrapping my decisions around them, I began to control the only person's happiness that I could—my own.

The next day, a group of us decided to take a hike with the hope of finding some good Swiss chocolate or coffee. We were at such a high altitude that the air was almost too thin to breathe. My face was bright red, not that I had verified this in a mirror, but I figured it was true because everyone else on our hike had a bright red face, dripping with sweat. Any energy we exerted in the Swiss Alps was worth three times the amount it of the energy that we burned at sea level. With that kind of cutting exercise, I wondered why the great marathon runners were all from Kenya rather than Switzerland. Maybe the Swiss chocolate was to blame, or the dairy. All of the families up on the mountain had a few dairy cows grazing on steep slopes of grass, and the wind carried an aroma of cow pie, reminding us of our mooing companions.

"I wonder how they get the cows on to the top of the mountain," I heaved, as talking was difficult on the hike.

After a few seconds, Matt gathered enough breath to say, "Cable car."

Matt knew everything, or at least he thought so. He would squint his eyes in a condescending smile whenever he explained his take on the world. Any chance he could, he would bring up religion, just for the sake of arguing. Matt was an ex-Catholic turned atheist, which caused him to argue against theism, often contradicting himself in the process.

"I don't believe in a higher power," he'd state in contest.

Then, if I made a scientifically based case for the existence of a creator, he'd argue, "Well what about Allah, what if Allah is really God?"

"I thought you didn't believe in a higher power, Matt," I reminded him.

He'd declare that he didn't believe in the Bible, and then try to cite it to make a character judgement about Jesus. In the unlikely event that he recalled a scripture, it would be taken grossly out of context. This exchange went on as often as Matt could find a way to bring it up. He must have struggled with post-Catholic guilt syndrome, where his body wanted to run freely without God, but his conscience nagged him. Our arguments reflected his inner battle. Even though his unceasing contradiction infuriated me, he helped me realize another precious nugget of wisdom—guilt is some kind of prison.

We finally reached the top of the mountain and went in to the only open restaurant, 1000 feet above our youth hostel.

Summer ordered traditional Swiss food, also known as a plate of various pig products, and I enjoyed some much-needed coffee. It was a jolly place, with big wooden benches and dark planks forming angles on whitewashed walls. Our waiter was a prompt man with a wool sweater and a lazy eye.

Looking in two different directions, he would ask, "And what would you like?"

Each of us would have to confirm whom he was addressing. When we needed anything, we couldn't tell if he was listening to us or to the old couple at another table, and so we did without extra sugar and utensils. There are some professions that people with lazy eyes should just avoid: waiter, teacher, camp counselor, or really anything that requires calling on individuals in a group without using their first names.

We finished our meal with a yogurt from the guesthouse down the hill. No one worked at the guesthouse during the day, so purchases were paid by the honor system. Lodgers could pick homemade dairy products and make change for themselves with a jar of money on the front desk. The owner's trust in humanity was walking a fine line between hopeful and insane.

In town, a ninety-year-old woman ran errands in a purple dress. She was an inspiration, and I couldn't decide what I most admired—that she walked around without help or that she still wore purple dresses. Summer and I had heard that the human life expectancy was supposed to be 120, when properly cared for. We decided that we would both live to be 120.

"I think the secret is having a will to live," Summer supposed.

"Okay," I replied. "Well, I have the will to live that long, so what do you say, when our husbands die and we're old ladies, do you want to backpack around Europe again?"

"Sure," she replied. "We can be roommates again and we'll offer nurturing advice to 90-year-olds, like the Gimmewald purple-dress lady. That young whippersnapper."

That night the owners of the hostel left, trusting us to take care of it until the morning. In all, there were ten lodgers, mostly Americans. It felt like we had paid only fifteen dollars to rent a huge cabin in the mountains, and it came complete with friends. There was no television.

"You know," I said, "it has been two months since I have watched television. Celebrity gossip means nothing to me."

"Well, I can get you up to speed on a few things," Steve offered. "For one, Lance Armstrong is dating Cheryl Crow. Apparently he's strong enough to be her man."

"Oh that was so stupid that it was funny!" I said. "Yeah, I guess winning the Tour de France five times and beating cancer does qualify you as strong. We all finally know what she meant now. What else is going on?"

"Unfortunately, Willie Nelson died," Steve reported.

"Oh no. What happened?" I asked.

"He was playing on the road again," Steve said, cracking at his delivery.

The room was full of fun. We lived in a forgotten manner, there in the cabin. Summer played chopsticks on the piano as Steve showed us a peculiar dance he invented. Earthy hikers told stories, which I enjoyed until they began to explain all the details of the Texas Chainsaw Massacre. The odds were much greater that I die in a freak cable car accident than at the hands of a serial killer, but there, in the dark cabin, I was certain that one of the hikers would prove to be an axe murderer. Unable to sleep, I waited with open eyes for Summer to come back to our room. She didn't show until the middle of my axe-murderer nightmare, scaring the living crap out of me.

The next morning I knew why she had entered our room in the wee hours—Summer had stayed up talking to Matt.

"Do you like him?" I asked.

"Yes," she said, looking a little dreamy. "He just stood out. Crystal, I knew from the moment I first met him that we had a connection. Everybody listened to his great stories, and I felt special that a guy like that was interested in me."

"I thought that Matt was a jerk," I said, without censoring my opinion.

As a friend, I probably should have been more tactful, but I was still upset about his disagreeable attitude from the day before. My opinion did not stop Summer from spending time with Matt. For the next two days, he was always hugging her neck or grabbing her hips. Other people in the hostel were even giving them relationship advice. One time, he asked me to take their photo and posed in a position that looked like a newspaper engagement announcement. In the morning he woke her up by jumping on top of her and gave her advice about how she should wear her hair, and the makeup styles that he preferred.

"You know," I said to Matt, "you say that guys prefer girls without makeup, but I don't think that's true. When I wear nice red lipstick, I get twice as much attention from guys as the times when I wear no makeup."

"I don't want my women to wear makeup," he said.

Normally I would leave it at that, but for some reason I wanted to push the envelope. It was time that I conquered my fear of confrontation.

"The only reason guys, you included, want their women to look plain is an issue of personal insecurity and control," I declared.

I expected him to argue even more, but he didn't. My test was successful. I approached conflict without flinching.

Matt was considering joining us in Austria when we headed to the train station. On the way there, he began picking lint off of Summer's shirt and cooing at her in baby talk. Summer could not conceal her discomfort. She wore a face that reminded me of Paris and the ferry to Greece, and I thought that she might throw up on him. Suddenly the chronic attention that Matt commanded was not appealing. In a round about way, we discouraged him from coming to Austria so that Summer could finally breathe again.

austria

Heading eastward, we spent a few days in Austria. On our train to Salzburg, we met two Austrian musicians; both were very kind and spoke impeccable English. One girl was reading an American fashion magazine with Orlando Bloom on the cover. That was our first point of cross-cultural bonding. She and I talked about how dreamy Orlando was for a while until she tore his picture from the magazine and gave it to me—what a sacrifice. This stranger willingly went hungry while I feasted on the Kentish eye candy.

A while later, the air became foul with the scent of cow excrement from a village dairy. Wanting to continue our friendship, the Austrian girl dramatically sniffed the air and pointed out the window with a frown. There, in the presence of an enormous lake and edelweiss, I realized this fact: cow pie really unites people.

As we departed the train to find lodging in Salzburg, one of the girls, Elka, invited us to a private chamber orchestra concert in an ancient castle, an offer that we could not pass up. We made plans to watch her performance the next evening.

Salzburg was lined with cobblestone streets, blonde children, and cafés. Summer and I spent a few hours going on a progressive coffee run. By the time we reached our fourth coffee shop, I was on a caffeine high and began to uncontrollably sing any and every tune from *The Sound of Music*.

Wreaths with dried flowers dangled on pink and green ribbons, and the folks hanging them were sweet and contented. Japanese tourists snapped photographs of a chocolate display. Why did the Japanese people need a photograph of a chocolate display? Perhaps because it was special "Mozart" chocolate. Music was an obvious tradition in the Salzburg community and many young people walked around town with violin cases on their backs. Austria exuded a wholesome air. This was because the national movie was *The Sound of Music*. Who wouldn't be good with Julie Andrews lurking round the corner? As we explored a nearby park, I found myself bursting into spontaneous song, once again.

"I am sixteen, going on seventeen …" I sang. "Oh gosh, was that out loud, Summer?"

"Yup," she informed me, though not amused.

Something was bothering her, and I resisted the defensive temptation to assume that it was my fault.

After a few moments of downhearted muteness I unconsciously erupted again. "With songs they have sung, for a thousand years. Ah ah ah ah."

She looked at me with a face that was upset, but tried to muscle a smile anyway. We crossed a shallow river and trampled through a clean field. Sometimes Summer and I didn't speak. We had so much in common and could carry a six-hour-long phone conversation, but once in a while our individual issues caused our discussion to halt. This usually occurred when we were lost in a new city, carrying our heinous backpacks while on a quest for sufficient lodging. There in Salzburg, however, Summer just had the blues. Patiently, I waited for her to open up while catching a whiff of new rain. This park was bright green with thick foliage. It smelled like springtime in Oregon, and took me back to my childhood. Feeling the comforting pain of nostalgia, I understood why people wanted to live in Salzburg.

Eventually Summer shared her heaviness of heart. "I feel disappointed that I let myself get so close to Matt. Not that I miss him, but I guess I kind of felt trapped by him."

In support, I offered Summer another perspective; "Maybe it's not your fault. Maybe when he knew you liked him, he took ownership of you—like you had been dating for a year or something."

"Yeah, I guess that's how I feel," Summer said, a weight lifted. "When I gave him some attention, he just kept seeking more and more. A lot of guys I've dated have drained me like that."

"Well," I suggested, "maybe you are looking at the wrong kinds of guys. The flashy, life-of-the-party types are magnetic, but a lot of times they have an unhealthy need for attention. Some are naturally witty, but others are just plain needy."

"But I feel like they find me," she said.

"Then you should limit the time you let yourself spend around those guys," I suggested.

Often when we give others advice, it is the advice that we ourselves need to hear. As I said those words to Summer, I resolved to look harder at the nice guys who stood in the shadows. Both of us would be happier in life if we considered the men who weren't so visible, instead of just the center-of-attention types. Shy guys are a treasure to be discovered, and loquacious guys are often selfish. We sat on some swings, letting the new perspective marinate in our brains.

"Wow," I admitted to Summer, "I learn new things about life every day. I'm glad that I have one more relationship epiphany to draw from in the future."

"Me too." She smiled, this time without effort.

Every day we both learned more about the world and what we wanted, and I was glad that neither of us were making life-long commitments just yet. A group of children looked at us on the swings—two grown-ups with so much yet to learn, including the idea that swings were meant for kids. We got the hint and let the kids take our places as we headed to the big castle on the hill, in anticipation for Elka's concert.

"Doe, a deer, a female deer," I began as we waited for Elka.

Only a minute later I whispered, "Climb every mountain. Forge every stream." Then a little louder, with jazz hands, "Follow every rainbow, 'til you find your dream."

Just before I started the next part of the song, Elka ushered us into the concert hall. It had beams of dark wood and white Christmas lights, and just walking inside, I felt like royalty. The room was filled with older, wealthy-looking folks, and I saw that they had paid forty dollars for the concert—we were it watching free of charge. The orchestra began with Mozart, since he was from Salzburg.

When I was young, I played in an orchestra for four years. With lamentation, my mother told me that if I quit, I'd one day regret it. This was the day she had prophesied about. For an hour I recognized the tunes I had once played, and regretted that I did not still participate in the assembly of such exquisite harmony. My parents had spent money and energy taking me to private lessons and honor orchestra practices, and I quit because I didn't want to practice. Well, actually, I quit because I didn't want to carry my instrument to school like a nerd. Now, listening to Elka's group, I admitted that they were not nerds—they were normal people—and after the performance, we joined some of them for pizza.

We tried to make conversation. It was difficult because they were strangers. It was impossible because only one of them spoke English. Summer pursued any avenue she could, but ultimately failed when the three Austrians slipped into inside conversation that did not include us. One thing we did get out of the evening was a lesson in German. We would add the German language to our arsenal of quick phrases like "thank you," "please," and "I would like one of those." Thus far we knew simple speech in French, Italian, Spanish, Greek, and of course, English. After the strained meal, we said goodbye, relieved to be free of the language barrier. At least the meal served a purpose when we learned how to say, "Ich Leibe Hasselhoff," a good phrase, we decided, to bring with us to Germany.

When dining in Europe, I would often encounter a new style that I promised to bring back to the states. For instance, in Italy, everyone would finish meals by peeling an orange for dessert—perhaps the secret of their thin figures. Also, throughout the continent, men and women alike would stop into tobacco shops for a quick shot of espresso. When combined with a teaspoon of sugar, the thick black liquid tasted like candy. The last sip of an espresso was potent and grainy, a tonic that put hair on one's chest and sent them out of the tobacco shop kicking. This caffeine ritual inspired me to collect espresso cups from each country, and persuade my friends at home to drink the liquid like candy.

Summer was supportive of my fragile collection, and to my surprise, bought me an Austrian espresso cup as a gift. The cup and saucer were feminine, like Summer. They were painted with tiny blue flowers and green ribbon. She was good at giving gifts, something that I needed work on.

When I was a kid, I was raised in a strict religious home. We were so self-righteous that we refused to take part in secular holidays, thus rarely receiving presents. Now that I am twenty-three, I realize that my lack of gift experience has made me a crap-present receiver. My dad's idea of a gift was to bring home the unused toiletries from a hotel room, and have my sisters and me take turns picking what we wanted. A typical present situation went as follows:

"I want to go first," says Gabrielle, three years my junior.

"Fine," says Rachel, two years my senior. "You always get what you want anyway."

"I choose … the sewing kit," Gabrielle says, grabbing the colorful ribbon, without a clue about how to sew.

Rachel picks the shower cap. Jealous of her choice, all I can think about is how much I had always wanted to wear a shower cap because they reminded me of people on television. My hand extends, clutching the shampoo.

Mom, noticing my disappointment, explains the benefits of conditioning shampoo. " That two-in-one shampoo saves you a lot of time, Crystal!"

Satisfied by my mother's words, I take a sip of cola, my hands wrapped around the State Farm drink cozy I received at last year's gift presentation.

The tiny cup that Summer gave me was a great reminder of

the little Austrian lake village where it was purchased. Saint Gilgen was a town that locals recommended to us, and we knew that advice from locals carried a lot of clout. Our view in Saint Gilgen was vast and green, with mountains in the distance and colorful rowboats bobbing atop the surface of the water. It was chilly, except when a beam of sunlight caught my jacket in an undeviating ray that was meant for only me. The air was so peaceful that I could hear a duck swimming, its trail rippling like a strobe light. There was a mountain in front of us that had the shape of a gothic church, sturdy with flying buttresses. Traditional Austrian costumes dressed each storefront and folks spoke to each other in German, as if there were no other language in the world.

We had arrived in Saint Gilgen too early to check into a hostel, and instead brainstormed ways to pass the time until five o'clock. After a stroll along the waterfront park, Summer and I decided to rest on some benches for a while. Thirty minutes had passed before I was awakened by the sound of gravel crunching beneath the feet of twenty English tourists. Summer lay fast asleep. One by one, the tourists photographed the water, politely disregarding the two American derelicts napping in the open air. My eyes stayed shut, nervously sorting out the next course of action. If I arose, I might have to explain the situation, but if I continued to mock-sleep I risked being photographed and posted on a website by some clever computer geek. There, on the frosty park bench, I understood the everyday worries of homeless people.

In a way, Summer and I were homeless. We were drifters, carried by trains and living out of backpacks. We slept in different places each night and made disposable friends with our fellow travelers. There were some benefits to living this way. With disposable friends, there was a sense of comradery unlike anything I'd known before. Travelers just expected to hang out together, usually in a pub, exchanging stories. It was nice to enjoy an adventurous stranger's company for a time, freeing even. With disposable friends there was no agenda or expectation. When a disposable friend left, we'd meet someone else. We didn't expect to stay friends with everyone forever—after all, we were not eight-year-olds anymore.

Saint Gilgen reminded me of the musical *Brigadoon*. Brigadoon was a little town that never aged. It was stuck somewhere in the past, forgetting about the outside world. Surrounded by mountains, I could imagine Saint Gilgen forgetting about the world. The lake would lap up against mossy rocks, and the townspeople would trade milk and dresses and never have a need to see a city. Summer and I walked on an empty dock, gratified by our Austrian experience. We had no need to see another city in Austria, and decided to board a train the next day.

The Austrian countryside was gorgeous. A shallow creek ran into a plush hill, dressed with a million heads of broccoli. The water reflected light as if neon snakes were crawling on its surface. A partially balding man rode the open road on a bicycle. He was too small to see, but I imagined he must have had a bell. A woman on the train had been to the market. Her clear plastic bag revealed radishes and bananas. At the next stop she exited the train, bringing these groceries to a local hotel where a Maypole waved last year's ribbons.

Onward in the country a debate arose in nature to see who was more lively and inspiring—the clouds or the cherry blossoms? Both fluffed around in the wind, but the clouds offered a greater selection of shapes, thus winning the debate. In the distance a small town united, wearing red roofs and bowing to the tallest building of all—the church tower. One thing spoiled my view of the Austrian countryside—satellite dishes. I understood that Austrians needed television just as much as the rest of the world, but only to watch *The Sound of Music*. My eyes rocked shut with the sway of the train, and I awoke in the Czech Republic.

the czech republic

We crossed the Austrian border into the Czech Republic to find small, ragged towns lining the railway. Transportation around the Czech Republic left something to be desired. On our way to Prague, we rode on a rusty old bus for three-and-a-half hours. One of the employees on the bus reeked as if he hadn't washed in a week and had never even heard of deodorant. Worse than that, he refused to speak without flailing his arms about as if trying to attain lift-off. The ride had no air conditioning, so his sweat only became more pungent as the hours progressed. Summer and I were so thirsty that we actually drank baby food for moisture. Lucky for us, Prague itself made up for the bus ride.

Picturesque buildings with ancient spires created a golden silhouette of the town-square. Our hostel was right behind a cathedral that put Walt Disney to shame. Walking the streets of the city, I couldn't help but picture every fairy tale I had ever heard taking place in Prague. There was a jagged clock tower from which Rapunzel let down her hair. A tortuous stairwell led a prince to the room where Sleeping Beauty slumbered. In the ballroom of a castle, a grand chandelier illuminated the fabric on Cinderella's dress. The regal bricks of Prague preserved tales from the days of King Charles.

We happened to be in Prague for the World Hockey Championship finals—and that's when I became a hockey fan. One evening, when the United States was playing the Czech Republic, gigantic screens were fashioned around the old town square and everyone came out to see the game. Goals were hard to come by and represented miles of teamwork. The players maneuvered the puck behind one another and bounced it off of the walls in calculated craftsmanship. Lacking hand-eye coordination, I doubted that I'd ever be able to match the precision of these hockey teams. My team ended up winning, and a few thousand angry teenagers began chanting violent slurs against the United States. Not wanting anyone to catch our accents, we made ourselves scarce and went to our favorite coffee shop to sip cappuccino and sing along to popular love ballads.

With a slight prejudice Summer said, "Why does everyone want to listen to American music?"

"I see your point, but are you aware that this song is by the Beetles?" I grinned.

She nodded and replied, "Well, you know what I mean, Crystal. They hate us and pick on us, and yet imitate our culture and pay homage to our celebrities."

"I mean," she continued, "why does someone in Austria care about Britney Spears or Andy Roddick?"

Her point was valid. In Europe I had regularly been approached by unreserved foreigners who smugly defamed my country, making generalizations without ever having been to the United States. I remembered a time in Ireland, when Patrick spent several minutes lecturing the bus about the ignorance of Americans, all the while ignoring the fact that Summer and I were riding in the front seat. It was in fashion to expect America to police the world and then criticize our involvement in foreign affairs. Presumptuous antagonists quoted to me the same statistics, leading me to believe that they all pulled their perspectives from the same biased news source.

Further than politics, foreigners liked to tell me that Americans were uneducated and recluse, saying, "The vast majority of Americans have never even been to Europe."

This may have been true, but when I asked how many miles they had ever traveled from their homes, the average was about the distance from San Antonio to Dallas.

Aside from American-bashing, we had another thing to get used to—unusual customer service. After a long day of touring, all I wanted was a vegetarian meal. Spotting cheese ravioli, I smiled and pointed out the item on the menu.

"This ravioli is vegetarian, right?" I asked our waitress.

"Yes, yes it is. Vegetarian," she responded.

Minutes later the waitress brought me a plate of fish. Once again, I explained that I needed a vegetarian meal.

"I'm sorry," I said, "but could I just order something else?"

My new meal arrived after my friends had finished theirs, and when the check came, I was forced to pay for the tardy meal that I ate, as well as the fish that I didn't touch. Instead of getting angry, I took this as a free lesson in Czech restaurant culture.

My favorite part of Prague was the west end of Charles Bridge. The bridge was known for it's medieval tower and view of the little town, with its red roofs and charming street artists. It is amazing to watch a street artist in action. In a matter of minutes, these free-spirited paupers can turn a blank page into the replica of a celebrity. The bridge was also full of wooden stands where jolly ladies sold handmade jewelry. We were welcome to shop without the slightest pressure to purchase something. Prague became even lovelier when we began to socialize.

Greg was an Australian traveling the world with his buddy, Nick. We met these two at a pub in the middle of a heated argument.

"You always make me navigate this trip. You are such a lazy loser," Greg said.

"Well you are ugly and your breath makes me want to hurl," Nick responded.

"Oh yeah," said Greg. "Well no one wants to be your friend because you talk too much and drink like a fish and girls think you are a dork. Everyone laughs at you behind your back."

"Oh yeah," Nick said. "Well everyone hates you and it's no wonder that your dad left when you were a kid. I bet he was tired of looking at your face."

Now, if Summer and I ever argued like that, we would not be friends. Yet these two had some barbaric understanding that they could slice one another's character as much as they wanted and things would return back to normal until the next fight. Aussies were tough in every way.

Though I was revolted by their style of arguing, I could not help but agree with Nick's assessment that Greg was hard on the eyes. He had an eyebrow piercing that hung by a thread and made you flinch, as it sometimes threatened to spontaneously pop out. His hair was long and oily and gave him a face full of open pimples, which oozed puss. His teeth wore a yellow sweater and were given to periodic bleeding. Summer and I decided that the only safe place to look, when speaking with Greg, was his chin.

Nevertheless, we were amused to watch Greg and Nick. The

more beer they drank, the more testosterone-driven they became, as they proceeded to have a He-man contest right in the pub. It is a mystery why guys have such an insatiable need to be the king of the hill. They challenge each other to duels of the will, where they bloody one another's knuckles until the weakest man forfeits the game. Such ego contests are going overboard these days. When I lived in Texas, I often saw trucks that had been lifted so high passengers had to pole vault their way in. To which I say, "Guys, no need for a big truck, we're already impressed."

With bloody knuckles, the Australians went back to being friends, and our group grew larger with the company of John and Andrew, two guys from north England. John and Andrew made everything into a dry, sarcastic joke.

"Do you ever listen to country music?" I asked John.

"Only when I'm suicidal," he responded. "Your president likes that kind of music, doesn't he? Maybe that's what gave him brain damage. What a pity."

"Hey," I said, "not everyone who listens to country music is stupid."

"That's true," he responded. "Some are bigots."

"I know that deep down you like American music. You watch Britney Spears videos, John," I said.

"Yes, I do," he answered. "With the sound off. But seriously, those videos give such a false impression of American girls. You think they look like Britney, when they really look like blimpie! Present company excluded, of course."

"Oh, of course!" I said.

It was a good thing that he did not get personal because I had a few things to say about his teeth. They had so many gaps that I though I was at a shopping mall. They all faced each other like his mouth was having a tango competition and they were searching for a matching partner.

After only thirty minutes with the English boys, my abdominal muscles were begging them to stop making me laugh. John and Andrew were an odd pair. John was small and carried himself like a monkey, especially when dancing. Andrew had freckles that danced across his nose, and he tried his best to camouflage a round belly beneath his denim jacket. These two were not attractive, yet their zestful company was enough to drag us all into a mangy Euro-techno dance club.

"Come on! We've got to go chuck some shapes," John said.

"What the heck does that mean?" Summer asked.

"Dancing, with proper techno strobe lights." John explained.

He proceeded to show us some moves. Miming the action of putting away groceries, his hands distinguished an imaginary top and bottom shelf. Andrew joined him in a suspended turn that he called "the snake." With that, we made our way into the lamest dance club I had ever seen. It was worth the cover charge just to see what people were wearing. The title of "King of Fashion Faux-Pas" went to a Czech man with a handlebar mustache and mullet who danced feverishly in a neon green workout tank. The queen was a small brunette in a sports bra and jeans that laced up the sides.

I wanted to say, "1985 called, and Jordache wants you to model for them," but alas, I could not translate that into Czech.

We chucked shapes with our English friends until "Return of the Mack" by Mack Morrison began to play. The Iron Curtain had not only held the Czechs under Stalin's thumb, it had retarded their ability to distinguish which pop songs were truly lame.

It was nice to have new friends in Prague. They were eager

to meet up with us and revealed to us the secret of thrifty travel. For their week off, John and Andrew had taken advantage of Ryan Air, a company based out of London that sold ridiculously low airline tickets. Thanks to Ryan Air, Prague had become a cheap vacation destination for swarms of English folks. The airline might have also offered weekend lobotomies because any restraint of conscience the English had in their homeland did not follow them to Prague.

On one occasion I was eyeing a pack of English twenty-somethings when I saw one of the many beggars in Prague knelt down with a cup in his elderly hands. Unlike American beggars, who played upon the literacy of society, holding cardboard messages, the Czech beggars appealed to utter commiseration. Sometimes ladies would crouch on the street for hours, desperately rocking a baby. This took more energy than bussing tables, I presumed. The pack of English boys must have agreed, because the next thing I knew, one daring fellow sprinted toward the old man and hurdled him in a pitiless game of leapfrog. The oddity of it all made me laugh, and my apathetic reaction made me cry.

As we made plans to go to Krakow, Poland, our new friends offered a word of caution: "Poland is really corrupt. Keep track of your personals, and whatever you do, do not ride the night train."

Innocently afraid I questioned, "Why, what's wrong with the night train?"

"On almost every night train into Krakow, thieves gas all the second class compartments and cut open pockets and purses to steal anything valuable," our friend said. "They'll take money, cameras, anything that they find useful."

With that counsel, Summer and I made plans to go to Krakow, on a day train.

poland

Outside of Warsaw, Poland, the largest population of Polish people is Chicago, Illinois. On October 13, 1980, Rick and Carrie Stanczak added to that statistic when they brought me into the world. Though I don't consider myself a Midwesterner, Chicago is the place I spent the first eight years of my life. It is also the reason my mom sounds funny when she says the phrase, "I have a black bag."

Like most girls, I have practiced calling myself by other people's last names, in hope to someday trade up from Miss Stanczak to something like Mrs. Orlando Bloom. (Crystal Bloom. That is too cute.)

All my life I had dreaded roll call. A teacher would flow through last names like Jones and Smith, and then my nose would crunch up with uneasiness. My strange Polish name with the silent letters was up next, and it would take so long for the teacher to spit it out that everyone in class would stop chatting and stare right at me.

"Crystal Sta ... Stan ... Crystal Stank-ca ... zack," the

teacher would say while boys chuckled behind me.

There were always follow up questions that mortified me.

"How do you say it?" the teacher would ask.

Thirty pairs of eyes watching me, waiting for the answer, I would correct her.

"Now, what kind of last name is that?" she'd ask.

With a defeated exhale, I would mumble, "It's Polish."

Then the teacher would write a note on her sheet, a note she would forget about the next day when it all happened again. Because of roll call, every kid who knew a Polish joke would use me as his test audience.

Later, I calculated a way to avoid the roll-call fiasco. Once any teacher got to the mid-Ns, my ears would perk up and I'd place my hand on my desk. Then, as soon as I heard my first name, I'd interrupt the teacher and raise my hand. The process was successful unless some cruel social studies teacher wanted to use my last name to brush up on his linguistics on the first day of school. That set the tone for the school year, and reminded me, as well as everyone else in a sea of Smiths and Adams, that my last name was just weird.

We stepped off of the train in Krakow, Poland, and were greeted by a teeny dark-haired woman named Anita.

"You arrive on train?" Anita asked. "People steal purse?"

"No, not this time," I said.

"Yes, you need to watch purse on trains," she said.

Thanks for the tip, but we're off the train, lady, I thought to myself, hoping she would go away.

"You need accommodation?" She asked.

"Yes," Summer responded.

Anita followed us around the train station, insisting that we rent a room from her. I was angry that Summer had said yes without consulting me. Anita was a pest, and the room might be a scam, and it was all Summer's fault. Anita led us down a dirty street, promising that we were near the town-square. Right in front of us, a nun glared at a homeless man who was relieving himself on a brick building. Anita unlocked three deadbolts and let us into a barren apartment.

"There is tourist here," Anita said with her best sales pitch. "Mexican tourist stay other room."

It was amazing what we could accomplish with hand gestures. We decided to take the room, and luckily, it was not a scam. In fact, I ate some crow when it ended up being inexpensive and near the heart of Krakow. The only unpleasant thing about the room occurred when I caught one of our hairy Mexican tourist roommates walking around the kitchen in dingy brief underwear.

"Sorry, sorry," he uttered.

"No, I am the sorry one, sorry that I have to carry that mental picture with me into eternity. Thanks, buddy," I responded, confident that he didn't understand me.

Dry heaving, I went back into the room, where Summer was still waking up. Seldom in our trip did we separate, but since I had at least forty minutes until Summer was ready, I walked by myself to a little park to people watch.

A little girl hopped around in piggy tails and shiny black shoes. Her parents were speaking Polish really quickly and eating fast food. Somehow I thought that Poland would have Sausage King instead of McDonalds, but now I know that corporations span every culture. Soft rain tapped the skinny trees over my head, washing the park clean. A lady with a stroller, two art students, and then a pair of nineteen-year-old monks walked past me. The people had kind faces, and went along with their business independently. A young nun sat on the bench across from me and I wondered what caused her to choose that kind of a life. Maybe it was in fashion to dedicate one's life to the Catholic Church in Krakow because this was the Pope's hometown. With that, I went back to our rented room so that Summer and I could see the sights.

Around Krakow there were many signs that ended in "czak." For once in my life, the "czak" letter combination was more common than "Smith" was. With joy I'd point out the different signs and tell Summer what I thought they meant.

"See that one, there," I said to Summer. "Kurczak. I bet that means son of power and wrath. Or maybe it means fine warrior."

"Or maybe it means chicken," she replied.

"No! No!" I said. "How could it mean chicken? It has to mean valiant prince or eminent horseman."

"Well, I think it means chicken, because it is an advertisement for that chicken stand," Summer said. "See, roasted chicken for two Zloty."

"Oh yeah, huh," I said, downtrodden.

At noon, we were on Wawel Hill, exploring a castle and an old church. The churches in Europe are like museums. They have tombs dedicated to locally famous dead people and artwork that no one would ever hang in a house. The townspeople don't attend church, so touring Japanese Buddhists see the creepy statues of monks with babies more often than European Catholics. From the hill we watched a wide river flow through Krakow, and then went to an Indian restaurant for dinner.

Our server, Magda, had light-brown hair and blue eyes. She wore thick black eyeliner that extended outward to give her an Asian look, but she wasn't fooling anybody. Unlike Prague, the customer service in Krakow was exceptional. Magda often checked on us, and when we only ate half of our enormous plates of food, the restaurant owner personally made sure that we liked it.

At the end of the night, Magda noticed the name on my credit card, saying, "You have a Polish surname."

"Yes, I do," I responded. "I am half Polish. Is Stanczak a pretty common name?"

"Oh yes," she said, and proceeded to give us a free Polish lesson.

By the end of the night, Summer and I knew how to say "please," "thank you," and "yes," and we could even correctly pronounce my last name, "Sta-nee-schak."

"And what does that word mean?" I asked, pointing at the word *kurczak.*

"That is chicken," she said.

"Thank you," I said in Polish, as Summer looked at me. "Just in case, you know? I thought kurczak might mean fine hearty meat or something."

Summer just laughed as Magda cleared our plates away.

Some time later, I was able to return Magda's hospitality when she asked me about Dublin. Like many Eastern Europeans, she planned to work in Dublin for six months in order to perfect her English. She didn't know where to go or how to find accommodation, and I was glad to set her up with a hostel in Ireland.

We spent the next day at Auschwitz. The horrific images of the death camp are still burned into my mind, and if I think about the victims at length, my face burns in sadness. Our tour of Auschwitz took us into a gas chamber where one million

Jews were murdered. The museum housed remnants of toothbrushes, glasses, and shoes that belonged to those people. One room was composed completely of artificial limbs. In their greed, the Nazis wanted to keep anything that might be of use to them. The artificial limbs were proof of the millions of crimes committed against the human race.

One tour guide was actually a Holocaust survivor. He must have had some courage to be able to face the death camp each day. I could hardly face it for only one day. There was a room in which photos were displayed of the first prisoners at the death camp. In the earliest days of Auschwitz, Poles were exterminated when they attempted to fight the German occupancy in Poland. Most of the prisoners photographed had Polish names. Stanislaw Ryczak, Stanislawa Adamczak. Names like these were common among my relatives, and I felt empathy for anyone who had lost family members. All of the hair had been cut off of the women in these photographs, so that they would be identified if ever they escaped. Cutting their hair also stripped them of femininity, and ultimately, humanity. One photo I saw was a fourteen-year-old blonde girl. She looked like my sister. Under her name it showed her date of arrival at Auschwitz and her date of death—she only lasted a month. When she was thirteen, I wondered if she had a crush on her neighbor. Did she like ballet? Did she pass notes to her friends in school? This pretty girl could have enjoyed a blossoming, full life if she were only born somewhere else.

Walking the grounds and seeing the wretched housing barracks brought me to a point of dismay. Summer and I spent a long time in silence.

"How could this happen?" I asked her.

"The human heart is a wretched and impressionable thing," Summer replied. "It is capable of more harm than we know."

Summer looked off to the side, at nothing in particular, and then she said something that I would never forget: "I guess seeing the very worst of life helps us to appreciate how much we have. I have a great life."

A few minutes before we left, I made eye contact with an Israeli soldier. We couldn't verbally communicate, but somehow it was understood that we both acknowledged the suffering that took place. For greater understanding, I spent the next few weeks reading the biography of a Jewish holocaust survivor.

We took a train to Germany and had very poor sleep because we knew that on the Polish night trains it was common for thieves to gas the passengers and steal valuables. I thought we were going to get robbed the whole time. About 12:30 a.m., a funny odor entered the air and Summer and I climbed down from our sleeping cars to the open window. To avoid being affected by the gas, we sucked the Polish air as cement walls passed in front of our faces. Our cabin-mate either spoke German or Czech—something that sounded mean. He wasn't wearing pants, but that didn't stop him from ripping off his covers and abruptly shutting the window. My alarm sounded every hour so that I could check the status of our baggage. After the third watch, we arrived in Germany.

germany

It was difficult to enter Germany without some resentment for the crimes that occurred during World War II. Truly, the German people have learned from that time and continue to educate their youth about the Holocaust; however, I couldn't help but do the math. If someone was a Nazi soldier in 1943, at age 19, they would now be 80 years old—still quite a lively age. I walked around skeptical of anyone over the age of 50, wondering if they still harbored anti-Semitic feelings.

Germany was attractive, but in a clinical way. The bushes were trimmed and storefront windows had a sterile shine, and I imagined that at night, men in white aprons inspected them with cotton swabs. The only thing that made Germany personal was staying with Sally and James Johnson, an American family doing mission work in Cologne.

Awkward is a word that I like using because it even flows from your mouth in an awkward fashion. I find this word especially enjoyable when a room of stranger encounters a stale silence, tumbleweeds and crickets adorn the scene, and one uncouth gentleman says, "So … this is awkward." Addressing the awkwardness of the situation only adds to the problem. People erupt in nervous chuckles, which fade into another bout of noiselessness. Sally and James Johnson would never be so candid to mention the slightly awkward situation that comes with housing two strangers in their German home.

Summer and I were being eaten alive by the horrible exchange rate of the United States dollar to the Euro. Our outdated guidebook quoted prices at twenty percent lower than the actual cost, so our funds were running low. Back in February, some of our friends in Portland suggested we pay a visit to their relatives in Germany, and looking at our bank statements, this had become an increasingly good idea.

The Johnson's were gracious and welcoming, though in the house I could sense their bewilderment in regard to what they should do with us. Sally took us on a lovely tour of Cologne, which included the Dom, a chocolate factory, and some extreme shopping. We were grateful to be with a local, who could show us the hidden treasures of this German city.

The Dom is the tallest church I have ever seen. It is so overwhelmingly huge that visitors walk away from it cross-eyed, with cricks in their necks. As with every monument in Europe, the Dom was in the midst of a refurbishing and displayed all-too-familiar scaffolding.

"When the United States bombed Germany in World War II," Sally explained to us, "this was one of the only structures left standing."

The church became more of a lasting reminder of World War II than a working religious building.

The name Cologne sounds familiar enough. When I hear it, I think of the bottom floor of Nordstrom, where snooty prep school dropouts make a living out of ignoring people. No matter how long one spends getting primped to go shopping, the jerks in the cologne department will always toss their hair in superiority. If I waved ten thousand dollars cash in front of one of those cretins they would still only offer a sarcastic smile, all the while thinking, "That Burberry scarf she's wearing is so last season." Cologne did not have its origins in such classism.

A humble building between the old and new parts of Cologne, Germany is the location of the fragrance's original production. Hundreds of years ago, in building 4711, a family began to produce this concoction that acted as medicine as well as deodorant for all kinds of people. The product was such a common export from the city that it became known simply as cologne. To this day, you can still visit building 4711.

Sally dropped us off at 4711 for a day of shopping, and naturally, Summer and I were thrilled to test the scent that put Cologne on the map. We entered the perfume shop listing what we expected the cologne to smell like. Roses, baby powder, lilacs, and cherry blossoms were a few of the top assumptions. With complete trust, Summer eyeballed the green bottle and motioned for a svelte German sales associate to spray her hands.

"Ziss is meant only for refreshing," our helper stated as a potent vapor filled the air, landing on Summer's hands.

It is difficult for Summer to hide her true feelings. She is one of those girls who wears every annoyance right on her face. This was no exception. As soon as the sales associate left the room, Summer's nose crinkled in utter disgust.

"This smells like … like toilet cleaner!" she cried, and rushed to the sink for immediate rinsing.

My sympathies were divided. On one hand, I was glad that my fingers were not causing passersby to wonder if I had dipped my hand in a port-o-potty, but on the other hand, I was sad that my friend had trusted the concoction and had been let down. Either way, she took care of the problem in a sink that resembled a beer barrel.

The sales lady eyed us, not in an accusatory fashion, but more in the way of puzzled concern. This caused me to examine Summer, gleefully rinsing her hands. The beer barrel wore the same green label as the stinky bottle behind us. There was a pyramid of perfume bottles on each side of this contraption, all sporting the green label. Summer was not rinsing her hands at all! Rather, she had just taken a hand to elbow shower in the pungent German perfume. Needless to say, the rest of the afternoon an invisible cloud of sanitation followed us like a shadow.

As we walked the streets of Cologne, we felt the warmth of late spring approaching. It was nice enough to just wear my tank top, so I took my jacket off.

Noticing my gesture, Summer said, "Yeah, it's getting hot. I think I'll go get an iced coffee from that stand over there."

"Okay, I'll wait here," I replied.

While Summer was buying her drink, I decided to be bold, and approached two cuties with baseball caps. Travelers are ready to be friends, and besides, their attire told me that they might be Americans. Sure enough, I was right.

"Hi. I'm Crystal," I said.

"Hi, Crystal. I'm Wesley and this is Evan," one guy said with a smile as bright as the sun.

"Are you traveling around Europe too?" Evan asked me.

"Yeah, and before this I was in Eastern Europe," I said.

"Cool. Did you see Prague?" Wesley asked me.

"Yeah, Prague was great, it had the funniest dance clubs, though," I said.

"What do you mean?" Wesley asked me, wanting me to elaborate.

"Well, you know, people dancing to lame music from 1995," I replied.

"Oh, were they dancing all stupid?" Evan asked, shaking his hips around and laughing. "Show me how they danced."

"Seriously? Okay," I said, and proceeded to shake my arms above me like something out of *National Geographic*.

Just then Summer came up to the three of us with her iced coffee.

"Hi, guys," she said.

"Uh, yeah, so we're going to go now. Later." Evan said as they darted off.

"What just happened?" Summer asked. "Did they leave because I smell like toilet cleaner? How embarrassing! Oh, I could just die!"

In the midst of consoling Summer, I remembered that it had been a month since I had shaved my armpits. I lost my razor back in Spain and didn't even think about it because we were wearing jackets all of the time.

"No, Summer. I don't think that they left because of you," I said, lifting my arms. "I think they left because it looks like I am strangling a Sasquatch under here!"

We started laughing so hard that a German man made a drinking motion at us.

"Oh great," I said. "Now we're smelly, hairy, and look like we're drunk!"

"Who cares! Who cares what everyone thinks!" Summer said.

"Yeah, who cares!" I agreed, although, truth be told, I bought a razor before we returned to the Johnson's house that evening.

The Johnson's hospitality was rejuvenating—a great change from the hostel world. With disconsolation we left

Cologne and moved on to another hostel in Frankfurt. It wasn't until I was three months into our backpacking trip that I realized all the things that I took for granted about being home. Plumbing, for one, was dysfunctional in youth hostels. In mid-shampoo it was possible to lose all water pressure and be forced to lap water onto one's self from a rusty sink in the next room. When another lodger walked by, the sheer frustration from rinsing by the tablespoon nullified any embarrassment that came with being clothed in a raggedy towel.

Another discouraging detail about backpacking was the lack of new clothes. I had been wearing the same four outfits the whole time, and was so bored with them that I intentionally snagged a shirt, just so that I could justify throwing it away. I was also tempted to throw away my backpack because it continued to rip, forcing me to carry it like a baby until I had access to a sewing kit. With sorrow, I wished that my dad was there to bestow a thoughtful gift upon me—I could have really used a hotel sewing kit. Perhaps the backpacker blues had colored my view of Frankfurt, or perhaps Frankfurt was just as melancholy as I supposed.

"You know, I'm getting used to seeing you from the waist up," Summer observed as we sat down for a meal. "We spend a lot of time in cafés and restaurants."

"That's true," I said as we eyed the menu.

In Frankfurt, nothing was made without meat. We went to an apple wine festival for dinner and even the potato salad and coleslaw were flavored with pieces of bacon. The beer, I figured, might also have been brewed in a vat of lard, thus causing me to abstain in joining the throngs of Germans who tapped one another's beer steins every two minutes. The only thing more tasteless in Frankfurt than the food was the live music. Blocks away we heard a painful growl and determined that either the people of Frankfurt were performing live animal sacrifice or there was a Special Olympics karaoke contest commencing in the old town square.

We arrived to find a rotund, suspendered man with a synthesizer playing alongside a woman in golden pumps. This was not an amateur karaoke contest; these folks were actually being paid to sing for the crowd. As my ears began to bleed from the excessive microphone feedback, I pondered some of the mysteries of German popular culture.

David Hasselhoff. When I was in elementary school, the show *Night Rider* was pretty cool. On any given Friday night you could catch high school boys wearing black leather and talking to their dash boards as if Kit the car was responding. Then a few years later, the *Baywatch* phenomenon swept through America, causing soccer moms the nation over to get breast implants. At that point, Hasselhoff became a narcissist. He'd insert not one, but two music montages of his own songs into the program. It is my belief that his contract also included a running-with-no-shirt clause so that he got to frolic freely twice each episode—often to the sound of his own music. Now doing this on television is art, but his relationship with Germany took things a step too far.

When the Berlin Wall came down, millions cheered, prayed, and reflected upon the freedom that was finally available to Eastern Germany. With sledgehammers, enthusiastic men took turns breaking the physical object that embodied their oppression. All of this was a growing crescendo to the grand finale in which David Hasselhoff burst on the scene to sing "I've Been Looking for Freedom." German ladies had tears in their eyes. Maybe it was the freedom, but if they were crying for Hasselhoff, I would never forgive them.

Another thing that confused me about Germany was the

male exhibitionism. On certain subjects, social order is tediously intact. For example, trains. German travelers can plan to-the-minute vacation itineraries because the trains are so punctual. Each person has a seat reserved to his precise destination. On other subjects, however, like male exhibitionism, the social rules bend. It is completely appropriate for a man to stop in the middle of the street and pee in broad daylight. Summer and I were taking a nice riverfront stroll when, to our disgust, a hairy greaseball silenced us with the pitter-patter of his urine stream. He hadn't even pulled his pants up before he faced us, and turned around to walk away. It was clear that German men felt entitled to inappropriate public urination.

The tone-deaf performers interrupted my thoughts as they attempted to serenade the crowd with a Gloria Estefan medley.

"Oh the humanity," I said to Summer, who was still picking bacon from her teeth. Somehow, it was easy to say goodbye to Germany.

somewhere over the atlantic

The end of our trip came full circle, back to London. After three and a half months of traveling, my impression of London was much less romantic, and much more human. People were just living life—McDonald's, taxi fumes, and mall walking. Sure, I still loved watching the way the English commuted and related, but this time I was not intimidated by their accents.

Summer and I stayed a few days in the residential area of Notting Hill, where daily life is mimicked the world over. We stopped budgeting so that we could afford to eat in London. If things were not so expensive, I might have tried to stay longer. Maybe I'd become an illegal immigrant, just like the airport customs agent presumed.

After such a momentous voyage, the only way we could face leaving was in a rush—and that's exactly what happened. We woke up with just enough time to catch a ride to the airport for our 6:30 a.m. flight. After thirty minutes, our bus never showed. Not wanting to repeat the incident from the Madrid train station, I paced around to try and find another way to the airport. We hailed a cab with a few other people—hoping that the cabby would have a lead foot. Indeed he was fast, but not fast enough. At 6:25 I rushed to the airline attendant and breathlessly spat out our story.

Without sympathy the attendant gave me a cool puzzled look. "Of course you have time."

"What?" I wondered.

"Of course you have time, because it is only 5:25," she said.

I sheepishly looked at my watch.

It turned out that I forgot to reset my alarm clock to English time, and we actually got up an hour early. It was the best mistake I had ever made. Had we missed our plane, the only option we had was to marry John and Andrew for green cards and raise offspring with teeth so crooked that they had to ask for directions.

"I wonder what John and Andrew from England are doing right now," I said.

"Yeah, they were fun," Summer responded.

"And Sadie and Betsy, and Ben and Bret, and Patrick and Chelsea, and Adam, and Christian, and Matt and Steve, and Greg and Nick, and Pablo and Marcos, and Anita and Magda, and Elka, and Phillipo and Paulo, and Sophia and Claudia, and Aaron," I added, "and Marcus."

These people enriched my life in such a way that I would never forget them. We were about to board the plane, and I wasn't yet prepared to leave all of these amazing folks behind me.

They say that you can never return to camp. Cabins might be there for fifty years, but the adventure and laughter leaves with the campers. Roasted marshmallows and fireside chats will only be recreated in memories. My mind would forever house thoughts and still frames of my treasured companions. When I hear "Return of the Mack," I'll always think of John and

Andrew. When I ride a bike, I'll always think of Adam. When I wash my hair, I'll always think of Chelsea. When I go to Starbucks, I'll always think of Marcus.

Twenty-three is an odd age. It is a time when unseasoned human beings are transitioning into careers, relationships, and adulthood with substantial pressure to have the world figured out. This tension between uncertainty and settlement is a crisis that most young people experience. However, the crisis can be beaten when it is used as a catalyst for adventure. When you take the time to get to know yourself, the pressures around you no longer dictate your position in the world, but rather personal discernment. Summer and I set out to see the world, and what we saw was ourselves.

Summer left Portland knowing that Sam was not her soul mate. Our trip, she believed, would help heal her broken heart. In the process she found her soul. She found the little imperfections that made her unique. She found the pieces of life that made her smile. She found what kind of guys she didn't want, and more importantly, she found what kind of girl she wanted to be.

I left Portland yearning to escape my life. Europe showed me that life began inside of myself. What made me happiest on the trip were all of the characters who passed through my travels. They had something special to offer, and I finally took the time to notice them. The same would be true about people in my own back yard. People are interesting, and I would be happier if I took the risk and let them into my life.

We flew over the Atlantic in dismayed joy.

"Wow," Summer said. "I can't believe we're going home."

Home. I was halted by the bittersweet dichotomy of leaving

Europe and reentering the United States. My feet had glided across Roman ruins and swanky Euro dance clubs, and yet I still felt a profound sense of excitement to watch my nieces at their small-town ballet recital. Back in January, Europe was something I had only seen in the movies. Now, I cannot imagine my life without the Eiffel Tower, London Bridge, Dublin, Cologne, Auschwitz, Chamonix, and a million experiences that grace my memory. They are more than my pictures—they are a part of me.

Slowly nodding, I turned to Summer and stated in all truth, "That was the best thing I have ever done."

And it was.

Printed in the United States
46430LVS00002B/46-48